The New York Times

POCKET
MBA
SERIES

LEADERSHIP
& VISION
25 KEYS TO
MOTIVATION

RAMON J. ALDAG, PH.D.
BUCK JOSEPH. ED.D.
University of Wisconsin

D0830464

LF

Lebhar-Friedman Books
NEW YORK • CHICAGO • LOS ANGELES • LONDON • PARIS • TOKYO

For *The New York Times*
Mike Levitas, Editorial Director, Book Development
Tom Redburn, General Series Editor
Brent Bowers, Series Editor
James Schembari, Series Editor

Lebhar-Friedman Books
425 Park Avenue
New York, NY 10022

Copyright © 2000 *The New York Times*

Published by Lebhar-Friedman Books
Lebhar-Friedman Books is a company of Lebhar-Friedman Inc.

Printed in the United States of America

Library of Congress Cataloging-in-Publication Data
Aldag, Ramon J., 1945–
      Leadership & vision : 25 keys to motivation / Ray Aldag and
Buck Joseph.
         p.   cm.—(The New York Times pocket MBA series ; v. 11)
      CONSTANT Leadership and vision
      Includes index.
      ISBN 0-86730-780-3 (paperback)
      1. Personnel management.   2. Employee motivation
   3. Employee selection.   4. Employee retention.   I. Joseph, Buck.
   II. Title.   III. Title: Leadership and vision   IV. Series.
      HF5549 .A545 1999
      658.3'14—dc21   99-27688
                                                                      CIP

DESIGN & PRODUCTION BY MILLER WILLIAMS DESIGN ASSOCIATES

Visit our Web site at lfbooks.com

INTRODUCTION

LEBHAR-FRIEDMAN BOOKS is proud to present *The New York Times* Pocket MBA Series, 12 invaluable reference volumes that are easily accessible to all businesspersons, from first level managers to the executive suite. The books are written by Ph.D.s who teach in the MBA programs in some of the finest schools in the country. A team of business editors from *The New York Times*—Mike Levitas, Tom Redburn, Brent Bowers, and James Schembari—provided their own expertise to edit a reference series that is beyond compare.

The New York Times Pocket MBA Series offers quick-reference key points learned in top MBA programs. The 25-key structure of each volume presents an unparalleled synopsis of crucial principles of specific areas of business expertise. The unique approach to this series packages academic books for consumers in an easy-to-use trade format that is ideal for the individual businessperson as well as an excellent training reference manual. Be sure to get all 12 titles in the series to complete your own MBA education.

Joseph Mills
Senior Managing Editor
Lebhar-Friedman Books

The New York Times Pocket MBA
Series includes these 12 volumes:

25 KEYS TO MOTIVATION

CONTENTS

KEY 1

Introduction and overview: welcome to the journey!

L eadership means "guiding on the way, especially by going in advance." The act is akin to venturing out toward a place where no one has yet been—an adventure, not for the timid, the cowardly, the weak. As part of the *New York Times* Pocket MBA series, *Leadership and Vision* will help you lead the journey into new territory.

Leaders are made, not born; they are molded by experience, helpful mentors, and opportunity. Most carry tools. This book's tools should serve you well as you shape decisions regarding your roles, the people that you lead, and your organization's potential.

Three themes summarize this book's contents: leading yourself, building productive working relationships, and creating and implementing organizational vision.

We hope you find our recommendations clear, concise, helpful, and, above all, practical. Not dreamed up in an ivory tower, our advice comes instead from a synthesis of study and experience. The suggestions are derived from some fifty years of experience with leadership research and consulting with business leaders of all levels attending executive-education courses at the University of Wisconsin-Madison and in companies across the country and world.

To lead others, you must first be able to lead yourself. Thus, as you read and lead, continue to explore skeptically both yourself and your unit of responsibility. These questions may help you continue your life-long leadership exploration:

- What are my strengths and weaknesses?
- What are the strengths and weaknesses of my unit of responsibility?
- Where do I need to improve my leadership ability?
- Where does the unit need to improve: productivity, quality, control of costs, safety, competitiveness, personnel knowledge and skills, morale, innovation?
- What are our opportunities for small and big wins?
- What should be our common vision and purpose?
- How do I inspire and motivate myself and others to support, commit to, and work to accomplish our common vision and purpose?
- What do I need to do to build a cohesive, productive team?
- What do the people in the unit need to do their best?
- How can we put more joy and celebration into our efforts?

Best of luck to you. "Bon Voyage!"

KEY 2

Develop emotional intelligence

A s adults in the working world, one of our greatest challenges is to manage our emotional lives with intelligence. Our passions, when properly managed, can help us to act, prosper, and survive. Mismanaged, they can wreak havoc.

Most experts now agree that IQ scores largely reflect a relatively narrow range of linguistic and mathematical skills. IQ taps only a small part of the full human intellect. Further, the skills assessed by IQ tests may be relevant to classroom performance, but the scores do little to predict performance in the "real world."

Consider one compelling demonstration of the need for an expanded view of "intelligence." At age 4, a large number of children were given both an IQ test and the "Marshmallow Test." With the Marshmallow Test, the child was given a marshmallow and told that if she could put off eating it until later, she could have two. Twelve to 14 years later, this measure of ability to control impulse was twice as strong a predictor as IQ of how children did on the Scholastic Aptitude Test. It also was a better predictor of adjustment, popularity, confidence, and dependability.

When people—whether "experts" or not—are asked to describe an intelligent person, they use phrases such as "solves problems well," "displays interest in the world at large," "accepts others for what they are," "admits mistakes," "is goal oriented," and "converses well." Such phrases suggest that people focus on the worldly side of intelligence, as opposed to just "academic" intelligence.

Howard Gardner, in his book *Frames of Mind*, describes several forms of intelligence, including logical-mathematical, linguistic, bodily-kinesthetic, visual-spatial, musical, interpersonal, and intrapersonal. Gardner argues that these are intrinsically equal in value, and that the degree to which people possess them helps explain how they learn and fare in the workplace. He further argues that it is possible to hone these intelligences, and that they wither with lack of use.

Only the first two fit into traditional conceptions of IQ. Gardner's "personal intelligences"—interpersonal and intrapersonal—are defined as follows:

Interpersonal intelligence: the ability to understand other people—what motivates them, how they work and how to work cooperatively with them.

Intrapersonal intelligence: the capacity to form an accurate model of one's self and to be able to use that model to operate effectively in life.

Together, interpersonal intelligence and intrapersonal intelligence comprise emotional intelligence.

As defined by Daniel Goleman in his book *Emotional Intelligence*, it is a "phrase for a different way of being smart. It's not the usual way of thinking about it—academic smarts—IQ—it's how you do in life, how you manage yourself, your feelings, how you get along with other people, whether you're empathic, how well motivated you are."

Emotional intelligence (EQ) is critical in answering questions like the following:

◆ Should you trust a coworker with a confidence?
◆ Is a friend on the verge of a nervous breakdown?
◆ How should you behave in an escalating argument?
◆ How should you respond to a racist joke?

There are many reasons why EQ is important in organizations, and in life in general:

◆ The emotional brain may "highjack" the rational brain. Fear, rage, and jealousy may prevent us from rationally addressing problems.
◆ EQ is especially important in higher-level jobs, including leadership roles. While technical skills may suffice in lower-level positions, the ability to deal with others becomes critical as we advance in the organization.
◆ EQ is critical for working in groups.
◆ EQ is needed to effectively manage diversity.

◆ EQ helps us adapt to new situations.

Emotional intelligence requires a rich set of abilities. These include:

◆ Self-awareness—Recognizing an emotion as it engulfs us.
◆ Emotion management—Controlling reactions to emotion-laden events so that our response fits the situation.
◆ Self-motivation—Directing emotions to serve a desirable goal.
◆ Empathy—Recognizing emotions in others.
◆ Relationship management—Managing the emotions in others.

EQ is critical in the real world. In business settings, EQ is related to a wide variety of leadership skills. These are demonstrated in group performance, individual performance, and the quality of interpersonal exchange. Those with a high EQ are better able to do everything from bringing about meaningful change within their organizations to conducting effective performance appraisals. Throughout this volume we will address issues, such as managing stress, self-motivation, coaching, and communicating, to help you develop your emotional intelligence.

KEY 3

Manage your time wisely

The average life span of an American today is 77.3 years. Compared to the eternities of time that came before us and will come after us, that 77.3 years seems but a small dust mote in a vast universe. But it is what it is—the only true resource we will ever have is the time we each are allotted on this planet. The only questions, then, seem to be (1) "What is my purpose here?" and (2) "To what best use can I make of the time I have left?" Every second counts. Don't let it steal away.

Time robbers & solutions

Here are some commonsensical solutions to dealing with time-robbers:

Lack of Awareness. Some of us are so busy driving that we don't take the time to step back, stop, and see where we've been and where we're going.

Record for two weeks how you spend your time each day. Analyze the data. Identify your time robbers—disruptions, distractions, unplanned

Each person's life is but a breath.

***Psalm 39,* The Holy Bible**

meetings, trivial work, etc. Think of time as money invested to accomplish certain goals. Are you making wise investments? For each item on your time log, ask three questions created by Peter Drucker, the famous management guru: "What would happen if this were not done at all?" "Which activities could better be done by someone else?" "What wastes my time without contributing to my effectiveness?"

No Planning. Sometimes, people fail to see the need to plan, arguing that they really don't have the time to do so.

Planning at the front end can produce a great ROI (Return on Investment), saving lots of time. "Measure twice; cut once."

Set goals and objectives to be reached within specific time frames. Break out the specific actions that need to be taken to accomplish each objective. Eat the elephant, but only one bite at a time!

Overcommitment. If you have too much to do in too little time, the cause is a lack of clarity regarding priorities. You cannot do everything that needs to be done, and you cannot do everything as well as you wish.

Be realistic. Identify all the roles you wish to play well in your life: parent, spouse, friend, leader, coach, etc. For each, describe your objectives. Establish priorities among your roles. If balance between family and work life is really important to you, set your priorities accordingly. Resist the desire for perfection—accept reality and prioritize. Resist guilt—do what you can and let the devil take the rest.

Action Distraction. Rather than think, plot, and scheme, some people would rather act even though action may not be productive.

On Sunday evening, lay out your plan for the coming week, ensuring that each activity listed will help you take steps toward the fulfillment of your objectives within each of your roles.

Multiple Stimuli. Many of us are bombarded with matters that seem to demand our immediate attention—the telephone ringing, the knock at the door, our e-mail. The impulse is to react without thinking—to clean out the queue, to empty the in-basket.

Take a deep breath when confronted with another demand on your time. Decide if the investment will be worthwhile. Critical differences exist between matters of importance and matters that seem urgent but aren't important at all. Put your telephone on voice-mail during important conversations. Put a "Do Not Disturb" sign on your door for a period everyday. Delete your trivial e-mail.

Sort your mail into A = urgent and important; B = not urgent but important; C = not important but urgent; and D = neither important nor urgent. Toss the C's and D's. Work on your A's and B's.

Procrastination. Fear of failure or success, fear of the enormity of the task, fear caused by feelings of incompetence, fear of conflict or unpredictable situations, fear of the unknown—all paralyze us from time to time.

Just do it! If you must swallow the frog, you might as well do it right now. The longer you wait, the bigger and slimier it gets. Take on the most onerous of your tasks first. Divide it into doable pieces. Reinforce yourself as you take each step. Check off each completed step. Set tight but realistic time limits to accomplish tasks. Work off your strengths and delegate the rest to others who are competent in those areas where you are weaker.

Lack of Delegation. Some leaders fear that those who report to them are incompetent and unmotivated. Others are threatened by competence. Still others aren't aware of how to delegate for effectiveness.

Recognize that an important obligation of any leader is to help subordinates grow. That is best carried out through training, mentoring, coaching, and delegation. Take the time now to train and coach and then delegate. Do not dictate the "how," just the "what" and the "by when." Delegating without dumping delivers this message: you are interested in their growth—you trust them—they are important to the ongoing enterprise. In the long run, your time is freed to concentrate on the urgent and important matters that you are best fitted to deal with—strategy, the future, the external environment, the time of your life that remains.

KEY 4

Learn to manage stress

While the term "death march" is used in a tongue-in-cheek fashion at Microsoft to refer to the stress of meeting looming deadlines, stress is in fact a very real killer. *Karoshi*, three Japanese characters that literally mean "excessive," "labor," and "death," is a term given by the Japanese to sudden death from heart attack or stroke induced by job stress. *Karoshi* claims an estimated 10,000 Japanese each year, and the Japanese government has begun to pay annual workers' compensation to its victims' families.

Stressors are environmental factors—deadlines, noise, rules, demanding bosses, and the like—that raise stress levels. Stress is a physiological state resulting from stressors. It results from a complex set of reactions that cause adrenaline to course through the bloodstream and into muscles and organs. Stress reactions are mental and physical responses to stress.

Stressors → Stress → Stress Reactions

Not all stress is bad. At low levels, stress is an activating force, called eustress from the Greek *eu*, meaning good. However, excessive levels of stress—called distress—have negative consequences. Most employees already face at least moderate levels of stress. More than 30 million prescriptions are written in the United States each year for Valium alone, and over 150 million for all tranquilizers. So, almost any increase in organizational stressors is likely to cause distress.

Stress leads to an estimated 1 million days of absenteeism and $20 billion in workers' compensation costs each year in the United States. Stress is a cause of psychological problems as well as physical reactions such as ulcers, high blood pressure, backaches, and heart disease. It has been implicated in workplace violence ("going postal") and employee suicide. Total stress-related costs in the U.S. exceed $150 billion annually. In addition, stress is associated with high levels of dissatisfaction, absenteeism, and turnover. It may also result in a climate that stifles creativity.

Almost anything can be a stressor—job insecurity, poor working conditions, too much responsibility, job loss, office politics, family concerns, and so on. One very important cause is whether the individual exhibits a Type A or Type B behavior pattern. The Type A behavior pattern is characterized by feelings of great time pressure and impatience. Type A's work aggressively, speak explosively, and find themselves constantly struggling. The opposite pattern—relaxed, steady-paced, and easygoing—is called the Type B behavior pattern. Type A's are much more likely than Type B's to experience high stress levels and to suffer negative stress reactions, including fatal heart attacks. Another stressor is life change. Many common organizational actions—geographical reassignments, promotions, early retirements, reprimands, firings—can have tremendous cumulative life impacts. Moreover, jobs with conflicting expectations (called role conflict) or unclear expectations (called role ambiguity) about what an employee is supposed to do at work serve as stressors.

There are many signs of stress. Trouble concentrating. Working excessively but not effectively. Feeling that you've lost perspective on what's important in life. Angry outbursts. Changes in sleeping patterns. Loss of interest in social and recreational activities. Prolonged fatigue. Increases in smoking, drinking, and eating. A feeling that you just can't face the day.

What can you do about stress?

- ◆ Take it seriously. Act as if stress is a matter of life and death—because it is.
- ◆ Set priorities. Try to reduce Type A tendencies. Allow more time for leisure activities. Ask which tasks can be curtailed. Learn to say no.
- ◆ Get fit and stay fit. Exercise reduces tension and strengthens the cardiovascular system. Physically fit individuals are better able to master stressful situations.
- ◆ Let it go. People who have high tension discharge rates—that is, who can quickly "let go" of a stressful situation—suffer fewer negative stress reactions.
- ◆ Get a little help from your friends. Individuals who have the support of friends and loved ones experience many fewer symptoms of stress than do those without social support. If you are lacking social support, seek it out. Social groups, churches, and local support organizations are possibilities.

- Think positively. Don't dwell on the worst possible scenario. Treat a stressful situation as an opportunity to show your skills and abilities.
- Learn to relax. Relaxation techniques such as the Relaxation Response and transcendental meditation (TM) have been shown to reduce muscle tension, heart rate, and blood pressure. Such techniques involve selecting a quiet setting, sitting comfortably with closed eyes, and repeating a sound or phrase.
- Practice self-motivation and time management.
- Manage change—avoid unnecessary change and think through the cumulative impact of planned changes.
- Avoid self-medication. Those who deal with stress by treating its symptoms—especially by use of alcohol or other drugs—often find themselves in a downward spiral.
- Get professional help. Especially if stress is severe, seek out professional guidance. Most campuses and many firms have people whose key role is to provide assistance in times of crisis. Take advantage of them.

As a leader, you can do more than manage your own stress; you can help develop a less stressful work environment. You can do this by clarifying expectations, providing needed coaching and social support, empowering, encouraging family-sensitive work practices (such as on-site childcare facilities and flextime), and teaching stress-management skills.

KEY 5

Practice self-motivation

As a leader, you must be able to motivate yourself and also to teach others this critical skill. Self-motivation is the process of motivating oneself. Instead of relying on others to reward and punish, to direct, to set goals, and to provide feedback, we must learn to use these tools to manage our own behavior.

Self-motivation is particularly needed when employees are relatively isolated, such as with telecommuting. It may also be useful when supervision is lacking or when employees must be self-directing, as with enriched jobs and self-managed work teams.

Self-motivation works. Early evidence came from clinical settings, where these techniques have been very successful in programs dealing with weight loss, smoking cessation, and phobia reduction. In academic settings, they have led to improved study habits and enhanced academic performance. In organizational settings, they have

He is most powerful who has power over himself

Seneca

reduced absenteeism, increased satisfaction with work, enhanced commitment to the organization, and improved task performance.

Here are concrete steps to take to change or maintain behaviors:

- Pinpoint the specific behavior you want to change or maintain. One way to do this is through self-observation. You may decide, for instance, that you are working on jobs that you should delegate to others, or that you spend too much time chatting with people who walk into your office.
- Set specific goals for behavioral change.
- Keep track of the frequency, duration, and any other dimensions of interest—such as the time and place the behavior occurs. Use diaries, graphs, or timing devices as needed. Sometimes, self-monitoring itself is sufficient to change the behavior. For instance, if you really identify how much

time you spend watching television, you may simply watch less.

◆ Modify cues. Sometimes the behavior we want to change is preceded by other events that serve as cues or signals for the behavior. By altering or controlling the cues you may be able to change the behavior. For example, you may find that you can't get your work done because you're constantly answering the phone. A solution might be to activate your voice mail or have an assistant hold calls. Or, you may increase desired behaviors by as simple a prompt as a to-do list.

◆ Modify consequences. This can involve self-reward and/or self-punishment. You might, for example, reward yourself for quitting smoking by spending the savings on purchases of musical recordings. Or, you may decide that you'll skip a concert if you don't meet your goal.

◆ Reorder behavior. We often do relatively enjoyable tasks in order to put off others we don't care for. As a result, the things we put off may never get done, or may get done poorly. To prevent this, make pleasant behaviors depend on completion of the noxious task. For instance, if you enjoy reading your mail but find writing reports to be unpleasant, put off reading the mail until you have finished the project reports.

◆ Write a contract with yourself. In the contract, specify the behavior you will change, the length of the contract, how you will monitor progress, the rewards and/or punishments you will use, and so on. Write the contract clearly and post it in a conspicuous spot. Have others witness the contract, sign it, and agree to help monitor your behaviors.

- ◆ Rehearse. Physically or mentally practice activities before you actually perform them. Rehearsal may suggest that you should rethink your goals.
- ◆ Check your progress on a regular basis. If you're not doing as well as you'd like, take corrective action, such as changing, or rewards, or making sure that you are rewarding yourself promptly.
- ◆ Plan strategies to maintain a successful change. If not, you may fall back into your old habits. But don't become wedded to the same system of rewards and punishments that you relied on to bring about the change. Consider something like a maintenance diet or give yourself a bit more slack regarding leisure activities.

Apply self-motivation to your own behaviors. Try it first with a behavior that you can easily observe where you may quickly see results, like an exercise schedule or a program to cut down on distractions at work. Then, apply it to a longer-term goal, such as learning a new skill. Once you master these techniques, you can draw on them to help with almost any task.

KEY 6

Leaders aren't born that way

A "born leader" suggests that some people naturally have the traits needed for effective leadership. What are the traits of a "born leader"? How are these leaders similar: Mahatma Gandhi, Martin Luther King, Chief Blackhawk, Golda Meir, John Kennedy, Walt Disney, Margaret Thatcher, and Napoleon Bonaparte? How do they differ?

These questions have tantalized managers and researchers for more than a century. In fact, the earliest leadership research sought to isolate the traits of "great men." Leadership qualities were inherited, many experts assumed, especially by males of the upper class. Thousands of studies have now explored leadership traits. Some of those traits relate to physical factors, some to ability, many to personality, and still others to social characteristics. The search for traits of effective leaders has proven elusive. It is now clear that the importance of particular leader traits depends on the situation, the followers, and many other things. It has even become fashionable to conclude that traits don't even make a difference to effective leadership.

Some patterns, however, do emerge from the mountain of research. Shelley Kirkpatrick and Edwin Locke have concluded that six sets of "core" traits are enablers of effective leadership—they provide the "right stuff":

Drive. These are traits reflecting a high effort level, including desire for achievement, ambition, energy, tenacity, and initiative.

Leadership Motivation. Successful leaders have a strong desire to lead, rather than to be led, and they are willing to assume responsibility.

Honesty and Integrity. These form the foundation for a trusting relationship between the leader and followers. We will not follow people who are unworthy of our trust.

Self Confidence. This is critical if setbacks are to be overcome, competing interests to be resolved, and risks to be taken. And, if your followers sense you lack confidence, they're unlikely to be confident themselves. Confidence and lack of confidence are contagious.

Intelligence. Leaders need intelligence to formulate strategies, solve problems, and make difficult choices. Further, followers' perceptions of the leader's intelligence add to the leader's power.

Knowledge of the Business. Effective leaders have good knowledge about the company, industry, and technical matters. This takes more than intelligence; it takes a commitment to learning.

The good news is that these traits—unlike traits such as eye color, race, or gender—are generally not fixed at birth. To hone each of them:

Drive. Do all you can to keep your energy up—get enough sleep, watch your diet, exercise, and manage your stress. Aim high—set "stretch" goals for yourself. Persevere. "You become a champion by fighting one more round," said "Gentleman Jim" Corbett. "When things are tough, you fight one more round."

Leadership Motivation. Think of yourself as a leader even when you're not in formal leadership roles. Take advantage of opportunities to lead. Volunteer for leadership roles. Focus on the benefits of leadership. Remember the words of storyteller Lewis Grizzard: "Life is like a dogsled team. If you ain't the lead dog, the scenery never changes."

Honesty and Integrity. Consciously choose to be honest and ethical. Anticipate situations where your honesty and integrity may be challenged, and think about how you'd deal with them. Constantly question your own integrity (see Key 13).

Self-Confidence. Arthur Ashe, the tennis champion, said, "One important key to success is self-confidence. An important key to self-confidence is preparation." Quite simply, you are more confident when you've given yourself good reason to be confident. Develop positive thinking. Life is a self-fulfilling prophecy—if you say, "I can't do it," you can't. Avoid negative self-talk. Don't think about the worst possible outcomes, and don't mentally beat yourself up if something goes wrong.

Intelligence. You can't will yourself to a higher IQ, but you can take advantage of your innate intelligence. Place yourself in situations that require your particular intellectual skills. Take the time to think through problems. Try not to make decisions in the heat of the moment. Apply your full intelligence, including your emotional intelligence.

Knowledge of the Business. Treat learning the business as a goal and challenge. Take advantage of education and training opportunities. Build job rotation into your career planning. Be open to learning.

These traits certainly don't guarantee success—success will depend on how you behave as a leader. Still, traits such as drive, the desire to lead, task-related knowledge, and self-confidence certainly help. They are enablers, your leadership muscles. You need to develop them, and then to use them in the right ways. You need to couple the right stuff with the right skills.

KEY 7

Make yourself into a leader

The relatively small list of traits linked to leader effectiveness may seem discouraging. To the contrary, we find it liberating. It suggests that it isn't so much who a leader *is* but what a leader *does* that matters. The question then is, what should a leader do?

For about half a century, researchers have examined a wide variety of leader behaviors, and one conclusion is clear: effective leaders show concern for both the task and the people they lead. Without concern for the task, the job won't get done. Without concern for people, satisfaction, motivation, and team spirit will plummet and performance will ultimately suffer.

Two sets of leader behaviors—consideration and initiation—address these concerns.

1. Consideration is behavior that shows friendship, mutual trust, respect, and warmth. Considerate leaders are friendly

and approachable, look out for the personal welfare of team members, back up the members in their actions, and find time to listen to them.

2 Initiation is behavior that helps clarify the task and get the job done. Initiating leaders provide definite standards of performance, set goals, organize work, emphasize meeting deadlines, and coordinate the work of team members.

There is no tradeoff between consideration and initiation—skillful leaders can exhibit both sets of behaviors. Should you as a leader exhibit both? The answer is that you should exhibit them *as needed.* For example, if team members are highly motivated, know their jobs, and have worked well together in the past, initiation may not help much. It may, in fact, be resented. The key is that you must show concern for people and the task, assess the situation, and then draw on your arsenal of behaviors as needed.

These people- and task-oriented behaviors are critical to the effective functioning of teams. When we think about great leaders, though, we usually picture something more; we expect inspiration, conviction, and vision. These are the essence of transformational leadership. Transformational leadership is based in the personal values, beliefs, and qualities of the leader. Transformational leaders broaden and elevate the interests of their followers, generate awareness and acceptance of the purposes and mission of the group, and stir followers to look beyond their own interests for the interests of others. Transformational leaders display five sets of behaviors:

1 Attributed charisma. Charisma is a Greek

word meaning divinely-inspired gift. More than 60 years ago, Max Weber wrote that charismatic leaders "reveal a transcendent mission or course of action which may be itself appealing to the potential followers, but which is acted upon because the followers believe their leader is extraordinarily gifted." Mary Kay Ash of Mary Kay Cosmetics, Jack Welch of General Electric, and Herb Kelleher at Southwest Airlines are known for their charisma. Leaders are seen as being charismatic when they display a sense of power and confidence, remain calm during crisis situations, and provide reassurance that obstacles can be overcome.

2 Idealized influence. Walter Bagehot, a noted 19th century economist and editor, wrote that "Strong beliefs win strong men, and then make them stronger." Leaders display idealized influence when they talk about their important values and beliefs; consider the moral and ethical consequences of their decisions; display conviction in their ideals, beliefs, and values; and model values in their actions.

3 Intellectual stimulation. Intellectually stimulating leaders help followers recognize problems and find ways to solve them. They encourage followers to challenge the status quo. They champion change and foster creative deviance.

4 Inspirational leadership. Napoleon said, "A leader is a dealer in hope." Inspirational leaders give followers hope, energizing them to pursue a vision. They envision exciting new possibilities, talk optimistically about the future, express confidence that goals can be met, and articulate a compelling vision of the future.

5. Individualized consideration. Transformational leaders do more than just "be nice." They show personal interest and concern in their individual followers, and they promote their followers' self-development. They coach their followers, serve as their mentors, and focus them on developing their strengths.

Martin Luther King, in his famous "I Have a Dream" speech delivered on the steps of the Lincoln Memorial in 1963, sculpted a masterpiece of transformational leadership. He spoke of values he held dear—"the inalienable rights of life, liberty, and the pursuit of happiness," "the riches of freedom and the security of justice," the need to "forever conduct our struggle on the high plane of dignity and discipline."

He envisioned exciting new possibilities, speaking with passion of the day when "on the red hills of Georgia the sons of former slaves and the sons of former slaveowners will be able to sit down together at a table of brotherhood." He assured his listeners that "With this faith we will be able to hew out of the mountain of despair a stone of hope." He recognized the individual needs and perspectives of his audience members, speaking of the "marvelous new militancy that has engulfed the Negro community" but also of "our white brothers." "We cannot walk alone," he warned. He used words of inclusion, hope, and faith, ending with his vision of the day when "all of God's children . . . will be able to join hands and sing in the words of the old Negro spiritual, 'Free at last! Free at last! Thank God Almighty, we are free at last!'"

Few leaders match Martin Luther King. But to the extent that you want to be a transformational leader, you will need special skills. You must be able to scan the changing environment quickly and systematically. You must develop and transmit a compelling vision of the organization. You must understand your followers' needs and values to motivate them effectively. And, paradoxically, you must learn to share power with your followers.

We'll close with two important points. First, these ways of behaving have consistently been shown to influence team performance, the satisfaction and motivation of followers, and many other important outcomes. Second, these are all behaviors that you *can* change. You can, for example, choose to pay more attention to those who work for you, to set inspirational goals, to model the values you espouse, and to provide reassurance in the face of obstacles.

Now, get to work and make yourself a more effective leader.

KEY 8

All power is relative: building your power bases

Let's start by defining some terms. Authority is the right to influence others; organizations can confer it. Power is the ability to influence others. We may have power without authority or authority without power. Influence is the actual exertion of force on others. Influence is power put into action; power is latent influence. Control is the exertion of enough influence to change others' behaviors. We may have a lot of power, and even exert a lot of influence, without getting people to do what we want.

These definitions suggest that power is *latent*. It is a weapon or tool; it may never be used, and just having it may make its use unnecessary. Also, power is *relative*. The power you have over another depends largely on things such as your expertise or rank relative to the other. So, a leader may have considerable power relative to one person and little or none over another. Further, power is *perceived*: If I believe you have power over me, you've got it! Finally, power is *dynamic*.

Power relationships evolve over time as individuals gain or lose certain types of power relative to others.

According to psychologists E. P. Hollander & L. R. Offermann there are at least three general uses of power:

Power over. This is power used to make another person act in a certain way; it may be called dominance.

Power to. This is power that gives others the means to act more freely themselves; it is sometimes called empowerment.

Power from. This is power that protects us from the power of others; it may be called resistance.

So, as a leader you may use power to do more than just change the behaviors of others (though that is certainly important). You may also use it to help others act more freely, or to prevent others from forcing you or others to do things you don't want.

If you're going to use power, you first have to get it. Here are five primary power bases, first described by psychologists John French and Bertram Raven half a century ago:

◆ Legitimate power results when one person thinks it right for another person to give orders or otherwise exert force. There are a variety of sources of legitimate power. For instance, in some cultures, it is considered right that older people or people of certain castes or with certain characteristics should be given respect and obedience. Further, if individuals accept the social structure as legitimate—whether that social structure is the hierarchy of an organization, the status ranking in a street gang, or a country's governance system—they are likely to obey the demands of those "above" them in the social structure. Finally, people with legitimate power may share it with others. While legitimate power sounds a lot like authority, authority is the *right* to exert force while legitimate power resides in an individual's belief that someone else *has* that right. These aren't the same. For example, unless the people who work for you accept your authority, you have no legitimate power over them. On the other hand, you may have legitimate power without formal authority, perhaps because of your age or seniority.

◆ Reward power comes when one person believes someone else can provide desired outcomes or remove undesired outcomes. Your ability as a leader to make favorable job assignments, to recommend raises, or simply to praise may all yield reward power.

◆ Coercive power results when one person believes another person has the ability to affect punishment that he or she receives. Your ability to issue reprimands, to give a negative performance appraisal, or to impose sanctions bestow coercive power.

◆ Referent power comes from the feeling of identity, or oneness, that one person has for another, or the desire for such identity. The commercial picturing Michael Jordan and saying, "Be like Mike," is a concise and direct appeal to referent power. If you as a leader want to have referent power, you must behave in ways that engender respect and liking.

◆ Expert power is created when one person believes another person has needed knowledge. Doctors, lawyers, and computer specialists may all have expert power. As a leader, you have expert power if others see you as competent, skilled, and knowledgeable.

As a leader, you must build and draw on an arsenal of power bases. Recognize, though, that people respond to use of these power bases through one of three different processes—compliance, identification, and internalization. Compliance occurs when we do something because we don't want to bear the costs of not doing it (such as being punished). Identification results when we yield to someone's influence because of that person's attractiveness. Finally, internalization takes place when we do something because we believe it is "the right thing to do."

Identification and internalization are generally more effective in the long run than compliance. So, while we may get what we want by relying on various power bases, we may get it in different forms and with different long-term consequences.

KEY 9

Practice effective goal setting

Employees have many goals. They strive to reach quotas, win contests, please others, make it through the workday, or outperform their co-workers. Their goals are sometimes difficult and sometimes easy, sometimes specific and sometimes vague. The nature of employee goals and how they are set are critical. Goal setting is a simple and inexpensive, but very powerful, tool in the leader's arsenal.

Why are goals are so important?

- ◆ Goals let employees know what is expected of them.
- ◆ Goals can relieve boredom. Consider how boring most games would be if you didn't keep score.
- ◆ When people reach their goals, they like their jobs more and are more satisfied with their performance.
- ◆ Reaching a goal earns recognition from peers, supervisors, and others.

◆ Reaching a goal increases self-confidence, pride in achievement, and willingness to accept future challenges.

Here are guidelines for setting effective goals:

Be specific. Specific goals lead to higher performance than vague ones. In fact, "do your best" goals have about the same effect as no goal at all. Imagine a runner circling a track, shouting to her coach "How much farther do I have to go?" A reply from the coach of "Just do your best" won't help much. Similarly, "directional" goals, such as "do better" or "lose weight" aren't any more useful. Instead, a specific goal such as "increase productivity by 20 percent within six months" or "lose ten pounds in ten months" is needed.

Set difficult, but reachable, goals. As long as the goal is seen as reasonable, more difficult goals lead to better performance. However, employees must believe the goal is attainable. If not, they will reject it. Also, people pursue many goals at the same time. If they believe one is too difficult, they will focus on other, more attainable goals. Interestingly, when people face difficult goals, they analyze their task more thoroughly and are more creative than when given simple goals. They both work harder and work smarter.

Let people participate in setting their goals. This increases understanding and acceptance of goals. An important—and perhaps surprising—fact is that when people participate in setting their own goals, the resulting goals are generally more difficult than if the goals were set for them. These more difficult goals, in turn, are likely to lead to higher performance.

Give feedback on progress. Feedback keeps

behavior on track. It may also stimulate greater effort. A video game without a score would soon be abandoned. And, when people learn how they are doing, they tend to set personal improvement goals. The most powerful feedback comes from the job itself, rather than from someone telling you how you've done.

A simple rule of thumb might be, "If something doesn't matter, it doesn't matter whether you do it well." Goal setting does matter, so you'd better not mess it up. In addition to the guidelines we've suggested, keep these things in mind:

◆ Set goals for everything that is important in the workplace. If you set goals for some things but not for others, those without goals may be ignored.

◆ Avoid the temptation to set just those easy that are easy to set. Sometimes, we really care about X but, because Y is easier to quantify, we set goals for Y instead.

◆ Work to ensure goal acceptance and commitment. Unless employees accept goals as their own (that is, "buy into them"), and make an ongoing commitment to achieving them, the goals won't work and may even be resented. Employees must see goals as realistic, and must want to reach them. This is one more reason to let employees participate in setting their own goals.

KEY 10

Help others improve performance

Carefully, consciously, effective leaders create climates of high achievement and high motivation. They do so through their abilities to inspire, persuade, and influence; to align their staff to accomplish a common goal or vision; and to communicate effectively with all stakeholders. But how specifically do they help people improve performance?

Here are seven disciplines to start and continue those who report directly to you on the right track to high performance:

(1) *Match the right person to the right job, or modify the job to fit the person.* Set people up for success, not failure. Place people in positions and roles where they can use their gifts best, work from their strengths, and minimize their weaknesses. Like an athletic coach, experiment and see who is best at what and match the job to the person. Not all soccer players have the quickness and leaping ability to play goalie; not all, the

endurance to play midfielder. Not all people have equal potential to be outstanding sales reps.

(2) *Make the job personally challenging and important.* Most people respond positively to professional challenges, especially when they know they will be supported as they tackle them. Most also want to see how their contribution fits into the larger frame. Thus, with all your staff members, face to face—

◆ Clarify the vision for your organization and its long-term goals
◆ Explain your unit's purposes, the reasons for its existence
◆ Show them the importance of their roles in fulfilling the vision, goals, and purposes
◆ Challenge them to find ways of doing their work better, faster, with less strain

(3) *Clarify your expectations of them and their expectations for you.* Involve them as partners in a common enterprise. Conflicts are created and productivity is squandered by a lack of mutual understanding regarding roles, responsibilities, results, and constraints. Clear communication—orally and in writing—takes time, but it is critical to building a productive team. Be concrete and definitive regarding—

◆ Required duties and roles
◆ Responsibilities, authority, accountabilities, and boundaries
◆ Reporting relationships
◆ Acceptable behavior to customers and staff
◆ Results to be accomplished (goals, objectives, and standards)
◆ Amount and type of support needed and wanted
◆ Preferred work styles

(4) *Ensure training in necessary knowledge, skills, and attitudes.* Through mentoring, one-on-one job instruction, small-group training sessions, and use of outside trainers, give people the chance to learn the skills required to meet and exceed standards. Great knowledge, skill, and appropriate attitudes can be gained from mentoring relationships between new personnel and more experienced veterans of the business, perhaps even you.

A simple but effective tool for one-on-one instruction is the following four-step method, which was created during World War I in American factories and has since been used as a standard method to train people quickly and efficiently:

Step 1: Set the Right Climate

- put trainees at ease
- guarantee success to reduce fear of failure
- preview what will be learned and how
- identify what they already know
- interest them in learning the job—sell the benefits

Step 2: Present the Job

- take one step at a time—be patient—allow plenty of time
- tell them and show them
- model exactly what you want to be learned
- present at a pace the trainee can follow
- tie to what they already know
- stress the operation's key points

Step 3: Try out Performance

- have them tell and show you
- ask them to explain the key points
- do not assume "instant" learning

- correct their errors; reinforce their successes
- require practice to help them acquire unconscious habits

Step 4: Follow Up

- put them on their own
- check often at first and then taper off
- encourage questions
- encourage continuing growth, innovation, and adaptation

(5) *Build a feedback system.* People cannot improve performance unless they become aware of how they are doing. Without feedback, we cannot adjust.

Imagine going bowling. You roll your first ball down the alley, positioning it beautifully. But five feet before it hits the pins, a curtain falls over the alley, leaving just enough height to allow your ball to go underneath. You get no feedback—see no pins fly, hear none drop, and see no score flashing on the monitor. What would you do? Except for going down the alley to investigate the cause of the problem or calling for the manager, you probably have just three choices: stop bowling, assume a strike and move to the next alley, or roll another ball. That's what people do when they receive no feedback: quit, assume success, or perform the same act again, unsure if they are doing the right thing.

Instead, consider using something like the widely communicated symbol the United Way uses during its campaigns. It charts progress publicly by displaying a large symbolic thermometer, the campaign's goal marked at the top, with weekly updates visible to all. Similarly, effective leaders build systems to allow people to see how they are doing against standards and goals. Computer-generated daily or weekly results help people understand their progress. Using project-management software that displays Gantt charts—graphics that show the multiple steps of the project—helps make progress visible. Also, leaders regularly provide clear, specific, honest feedback on performance.

Review and coach them for improved perform-ance. Make it a regular practice to sit down with each of the people who reports directly to you to:

◆ Together, appraise performance against standards, goals, and objectives
◆ Receive feedback as well as give it
◆ Select areas to improve, one at a time
◆ Together, create improvement plans
◆ Coach to help implement the improvement plan

(6) *Reward performance improvements.* Rewarding people for improved results can encourage them to maintain or increase their performance levels. Although important, it's not so much the nature of the reward itself that is critical as it's a matter of being recognized publicly or privately for the per-formance. Someone noticed! But spread the notice around—in a sincere manner. When deserved, give credit freely when a person who reports to you achieves a performance goal, exceeds a perform-ance standard, or meets the standard that he has had difficulty with in the past. Reward your superstars, your steadies, and the people who are developing. Here are some possible reinforcers:

◆ Tangible rewards: pay increases, bonuses, job security, tuition refunds, promotions, etc.
◆ Psychic rewards: praise, increased respon-sibility, involvement in decisions that affect them, freedom and authority, job assign-ment, improved working conditions, greater challenge, etc.

KEY 11

Empower others

Elephant trainers take an interesting approach to teaching the elephant to stand still. They tie a thick chain around the elephant's leg and fasten the chain to a large pole or tree. Once the elephant has learned that it cannot pull free, the chain is no longer needed. A rope draped around a leg and dropped on the ground is sufficient to keep the elephant in place. Having fought without success to break free from its chains, the elephant has learned to be helpless.

Chains in organizations are less obvious but no less real. They take the form of inflexible rules and regulations, stiflingly close supervision, rewards that have nothing to do with performance, and meaningless jobs. Workers faced with this frustrating work environment become dissatisfied, lose motivation, and experience burnout. Anger or apathy or absenteeism may ensue. When management sees these consequences, its typical response is to make rules tighter, supervision closer, and jobs more constrained, accelerating the downward spiral of powerlessness.

Empowerment seeks to break this spiral by giving employees a sense of real control. Leaders empower by removing chains, developing subordinates' self-sufficiency, and employing empowering leadership practices.

There is an old Abbott and Costello routine in which Costello, playing a patient, raises his arm and says to Abbott, playing a doctor, "Doc, it hurts when I do this." Abbott replies, "Don't *do* that!" Step one: Find the chains that are binding employees and then don't *do* that. Cut unnecessary red tape, rethink stifling rules, back off on overly close supervision, and treat your employees as capable and mature individuals.

Step two is to develop the belief among your employees that they can be successful in accomplishing their assigned tasks. Of course, the most powerful way to convince people they can master a task is to have them master it! Sometimes, this is best accomplished by starting with "small wins." That is, give the employee a manageable portion of the task to master, or have short-term goals that can be met on the way to larger accomplishments. Also, vicarious experience—seeing others who have mastered the task—often helps. So, you might point out others who have been able to do well on the same or similar tasks in the past—"If they can do it, you can do it!" Similarly, videos in job training might show someone doing the task well.

Step three is to draw on an arsenal of empowering leadership practices. For example:

◆ Let the people who work for you participate in decision making. They will gain a sense of control over their work lives and they will be more enthusiastic about implementing the decisions and selling them to others.

- Offer control over work processes. Toyota, Saturn, and Jaguar let workers on their assembly lines stop the lines at any time if they have a problem, immediately correcting errors and reducing the number of faulty products. Similarly, many hotels now let their desk clerks respond directly to customers' concerns without having to get supervisors' approval; they can even void customers' bills, granting them a free stay to compensate for a bad experience.

- Tie rewards to performance. Employees naturally feel powerless when they see that they aren't allowed to make a difference. When they see that their actions directly influence things they care about, they gain a sense of control—and they're more likely to do it again.

- Express confidence, encouragement, and support. Celebrate "small wins" and provide assurances that obstacles can be overcome.

Unchain your employees and give them a chance to do their best. Power to the people!

KEY 12

Build effective teams

Today's business teams take many forms and handle many tasks. Problem-solving teams, such as quality circles, meet periodically to improve quality, efficiency, and the work environment. Self-managing teams may produce an entire product. Their members learn all tasks, rotate from job to job, and often take over managerial duties, such as scheduling, hiring, and ordering materials. Cross-functional teams are formed to monitor, standardize, and improve work processes that cut across different parts of the organization, to develop products, or to address issues calling for broad representation and expertise. Clearly, team-management skills are increasingly critical. Here are three guidelines for building effective teams:

Encourage productive roles. Team members may adopt many roles, not all of them positive. Task-oriented roles—needed to get the job done—consist of acts like initiating tasks, gathering information, offering suggestions, and helping to motivate team members. Relations-oriented roles—needed to keep the team healthy and its members satisfied—involve such behaviors as keeping the group harmonious, helping members resolve disputes, and encouraging members as they face barriers. Team members, however, may also assume other, self-serving roles. Some team members may gain a sense of power by dominating others or blocking others' attempts to get things done. These roles often hamper team performance and cohesiveness.

- Encourage and reward members who play positive roles.
- Recognize that both task- and relations-oriented roles are critical to performance. A team that focuses on only relations-oriented roles may never get the job done. A team that emphasizes only task roles is likely to face growing dissatisfaction among its members, lose team spirit, and breed disruptive conflicts.
- Identify and discourage negative roles. You as a team leader must ensure that disruptive, self-serving behaviors are not tolerated.
- Make sure that assignments are clear, messages are consistent and unambiguous, and responsibilities are not overwhelming.

Encourage effective norms. Norms, the unwritten rules of the team, communicate expectations about how team members should behave. Teams may form norms regarding how members should dress, how hard they should work, how much they should help one another, or whether they should keep secrets from others in the organization. Because we want to meet our team members' expectations, norms control our behavior perhaps more powerfully than do rules and orders. Members may "import" norms when they join the team. Norms may also develop because of some critical event in the life of the team. For example, if a major client stops doing business with a firm because he was upset by an employee's rude behavior, norms may develop about how to interact with clients. Often, though, norms develop gradually in the life of the team, after the team has passed through a series of developmental stages and experienced a lot of jockeying for position, testing of boundaries, and conflict.

When forming, team members get acquainted and become oriented to the task. They are uncertain about expectations and acceptable behaviors. At this stage, you as a leader can help members become comfortable and feel like part of the team. Encourage communication and interaction among members; help quiet members build relations with the rest.

While storming, the team is likely to experience conflict. Members become more assertive in their roles, and their real personalities emerge. The team lacks cohesiveness as people jockey for positions. This stage may be necessary to permit agreement and a common vision to develop, but the team must get past it to become productive. As such, you must help the team work through this stage in ways that are ultimately constructive.

By the norming stage, conflicts have largely been resolved, and the team becomes more cohesive. Members settle into roles; and team norms, values, and expectations develop. Here you can actively help members agree on roles, values, and norms.

When performing, the team has reached maturity.

Members have learned the bounds of acceptable behavior, worked through disagreements, developed norms, and settled in to their roles. The team now focuses on performance, constructively facing new challenges, coordinating its activities, and pursuing its vision. At this stage, the team can largely manage its own affairs. You can step back a bit, concentrating on helping the team with its self-management.

- ◆ Recognize the power of norms. While unwritten, norms are just as real, just as powerful, and perhaps more enduring than written rules and regulations.
- ◆ Identify team norms and reinforce positive norms.
- ◆ Shape norms by communicating expectations concerning performance and other goals.
- ◆ Because norming takes place relatively late in the development process, begin to shape positive norms as early as possible.

Build team spirit. Some teams "stick together" better than others, having a real sense of team spirit. Members are proud to be associated with each other and with the team. Teams with high levels of this team spirit—also called cohesiveness—generally are more effective in achieving their goals than teams that lack it. Members of cohesive teams also communicate relatively better with one another, are more satisfied, and feel less tension and anxiety. Cohesiveness does increase pressure for conformity to team norms. If a team has norms of high performance, creativity, and an honest day's work, greater cohesiveness is probably helpful. If it has norms of leaving work early, doing as little as possible on the job, or padding the budget, increased cohesiveness may not be a good thing.

- Make team membership attractive. Use logos and team names as appropriate. Emphasize team status. Make team membership an honor.
- Praise and publicize team accomplishments. Go for some "small wins." Success on these easier initial projects may build cohesiveness and confidence as the team tackles larger tasks.
- Don't make the team larger than necessary.
- Identify outside threats and pressures. Work with your team to counter them.

The way a team plays as a whole determines its success. You may have the greatest bunch of individual stars in the world, but if they don't play together, the club won't be worth a dime.

Babe Ruth

KEY 13

Practice ethical leadership

As a leader, it is absolutely critical that you behave ethically. One reason is obvious and overwhelming—it is the right thing to do. Another is perhaps less evident; if you do not, you will lose respect—of yourself and others—as well as credibility and trust, and as you do you will lose the power to lead.

Be honest, direct, and open in your dealings with others. Jim Kouzes and Barry Posner, authors of *The Leadership Challenge*, surveyed more than 20,000 people on four continents to identify the characteristics they most look for and admire in a leader. Only four characteristics were identified by more than 50%: competent (63%), inspiring (68%), forward-looking (75%) and honest (88%). Honesty's top rating suggests that it is perhaps *the* essential ingredient of successful leadership.

Take ethical stands on difficult issues. Confucius said, "The superior man understands what is right; the inferior man understands what will sell." The willingness to stand up for your beliefs is one mark of a transformational leader.

Ask if your actions reflect the rights of others, including rights like due process, free speech, and privacy.

Ask if your actions are just. An act is unjust if it involves unequal treatment of individuals or inconsistent administration of rules.

Be aware that no power base is inherently ethical or unethical. Referent power, which seems positive, may be used to get a teenager to use drugs or to induce a colleague to cheat on an expense account. Coercive power, which seems negative, may be humanely employed to stop an employee's self-destructive behavior.

Use your power in ethical ways. If you use legitimate power, make polite requests. If you use reward power, deliver on your promises. If you use coercive power, fully inform people who work for you of the rules and penalties for violations, provide warning before punishing, and administer discipline consistently and promptly. If you use referent power, take actions that justify and maintain that power: treat people fairly, be considerate of their needs and feelings, show your appreciation when they do things that please you, and defend their interests when acting as a group representative. If you use expert power, do nothing to endanger those relying on your expertise.

Apply the sunlight test—how you would feel if your actions were brought to the light of day? Would you be proud to have your children read about them in the newspaper? "Do not do," Leah Arendt said, "what you would undo if caught."

Always do right. This will gratify some people and astonish the rest.

Mark Twain

As a leader, it is not enough that you behave ethically; you must also encourage ethical behavior in others.

Promote, communicate, and reward ethical behavior as a key value.

Model ethical behavior. Both in public and private, act in ways you hope and expect others to act. If others see that you don't walk the talk, your speeches about ethics will be dismissed as hypocrisy.

Speak out against unethical behavior when you see it. Don't wink at it or ignore it, and certainly don't reward it. Remember that if employees can get ahead by acting in unethical ways and nothing is done about it, that behavior is being rewarded and will probably be repeated.

Communicate expectations regarding ethical behavior. Make sure employees are aware of the firm's code of ethics. A code of ethics is most meaningful when employees have a say in drafting and revising it. It should be a living document that embodies principles that show up in performance appraisals and the reward system.

Make sure that goals don't push employees into unethical behavior. Unreasonable goals are often the motivation for lying, cheating, and stealing.

Encourage ethics training. Make sure employees know about laws, policies, and expectations regarding ethical behavior. For example, Lockheed Martin Corporation uses mini-cases in a game called "GrayMatters" to educate its employees about ethical issues relating to bribes and conflicts of interest, workplace relationships and responsibilities, suspected dishonesty of coworkers, and other matters. Unfortunately, no more than a quarter of all employees in Fortune 1000 firms receive ethics training and education at least once a year. About the same number receive no ethics training or education of any sort.

Don't force employees to ignore unethical behavior, to accept it, or to jeopardize their careers by going outside the firm with their concerns (that is, by whistleblowing). Give them ways to voice their ethical questions and concerns. For instance, about half of the Fortune 1000 firms have adopted some kind of telephone-based system employees can use (anonymously if they prefer) for ethics and compliance complaints and questions.

Set up internal programs to resolve ethical conflicts. Develop clear routines and procedures for dealing with any complaints or allegations brought against employees under the ethics policies of the firm.

KEY 14

Communicate clearly

The ability to communicate—to create understanding between yourself and all your key stakeholders—is the single most important leadership skill to develop and sharpen.

If you are in a position of leadership, every word you speak, every action you take, and every decision you make are sure to be scrutinized by your peers, by those who report to you, by those above you in the organization, by vendors, customers, and sponsors. You cannot speak off the top of your head, blurt, or babble if you wish to establish and maintain trust with those you influence. Without sensitivity, care, and deep concern regarding what you say and especially how you say it, what you do and what you don't do, you can easily erode or destroy your leadership credibility.

But what exactly is communication, what elements make up the system, and how do you improve your ability to send clear leadership messages?

Communication is the act by which leaders create understanding, not simply that of sending information. Unless receivers understand your message in the way you intended it to be understood, you, the sender, are not communicating. No such thing called "one-way communication" exists, for to fit the definition, both parties have to understand one another.

Communication looks simple. Within an environment, a sender formulates a content message, sends that message through verbal and nonverbal channels to a receiver who translates the message into meaning and sends feedback to the sender confirming the understanding. Sure, the process looks simple, but each element of the system is very susceptible to noise. Here are some tips to reduce that noise when sending leadership messages:

Aristotle said 2,800 years ago that outstanding communicators must first understand their audiences and gear their language and persuasive appeals to them.

- What information do your receivers need and want from you (answers to who, what where, when, why, and how)?
- What language level should you use to ensure your audiences understand you? What motivates them? What appeals to them?
- What do they find persuasive? What turns them off?

To reduce sender noise, shift gears from the "I-attitude" to the "you-attitude." Communicate directly to your audience using the pronoun "you." Anticipate other people's objections and questions, and look at the situation from your audience's point of view before you communicate your message and seek to implement your goals.

True effectiveness does not come from a large vocabulary, well-polished platform skills, the latest in technological gimmickry, or a smooth, glib speaking style. Communication effectiveness comes principally from one's inner drive, one's motivation to create understanding. As one executive summarized it one day, "If you wish to get your message through the clutter, you really gotta wanna!" Most communication problems are caused not by errors of commission but by errors of omission, from people not taking the time and putting in the needed effort to communicate.

Be clear in your own mind first. Take your time. Be disciplined. To improve your clarity, write out your ideas, put them away for a time, and then come back to edit them once you are cool and collected. Words spoken in haste without thinking create problems that, at best, will mean spending a lot more time or, at worst, will leave you stymied.

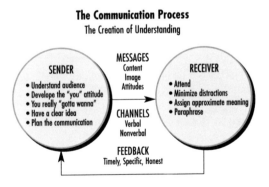

The Communication Process
The Creation of Understanding

SENDER
- Understand audience
- Develope the "you" attitude
- You really "gotta wanna"
- Have a clear idea
- Plan the communication

MESSAGES
Content
Image
Attitudes

CHANNELS
Verbal
Nonverbal

RECEIVER
- Attend
- Minimize distractions
- Assign approximate meaning
- Paraphrase

FEEDBACK
Timely, Specific, Honest

In summary, plan, plan, plan the communication:

- ◆ Clarify your purpose: Are you communicating to inform, inquire, persuade, inspire, document, or create or maintain good will?
- ◆ Define specifically the best-intended results for your communication. What do you visualize happening during and after? Set up yourself—and your receivers—for success.
- ◆ Define how you wish to be perceived in terms of your ethos—your character, values, and temperament. What attitudes do you wish to display toward your content, your receivers, and yourself?
- ◆ Define your audience in terms of language, their roles, needs, wants, objectives, questions, and priorities.
- ◆ Select the best time, place, and means to create that understanding. Is it best to communicate with an individual face-to-face or through e-mail? For a group, is a meeting really necessary? If so, where and when?

KEY 15

Lead effective meetings

What's the single greatest drain of organizational productivity? It is not when people surf the Net or take an extra fifteen minutes on lunch. No, it is attending unnecessary and poorly planned meetings.

A meeting can be described, as meeting guru John Tropman sees it, as a

> 'deal' between the members of the meeting and those who have called the meeting together. . . . the members expect to be treated well, to be involved, and to use their time in a productive manner. On the meeting caller's side, there is the expectation that the collectivity will act in a responsible way to assist in the development of a high-quality decision.

To ensure that this "deal" is a win-win proposition, leaders of effective meetings do the following:

PLAN THOROUGHLY

Decide, first, whether a meeting is the best vehicle of communication for your purposes. If you are simply calling a meeting to pass on information, don't do it. Use e-mail, reports, or memoranda for that. Have a meeting when you need or want people to discuss or decide issues together in those situations when you lack the necessary knowledge to develop a quality decision yourself. Another good reason for a meeting is to spread decision-making power among the group, or to ensure that decisions will be implemented with commitment because everyone who matters was involved in making them.

Ritualistic Monday morning staff meetings where people simply report to the entire group on the activities of their unit may be a cultural norm of your organization. But are they necessary? Do they enhance productivity and morale? Do they promote understanding, cooperation, and consensual decision making? Or are they marked by defensive game-playing, inter-unit competition, general and specific craziness, and showing off in front of the boss? Are they "games" or productive processes? If the former, consider canceling them until further notice.

For each meeting you run, orchestrate it like a professional. Ensure that the right people are invited, those who have the necessary knowledge, experience, and capability of actively and intelligently contributing to an enlightening discussion or a high-quality decision.

Choose carefully the best time and place for your meeting, ensuring that all logistical arrangements (room size, visual aids, coffee, food service, seating, etc.) are made well in advance. Ensure that the tables and chairs in the meeting room are arranged for maximum participation. A U-shape, box, or an oval around a large table work well for open discussions. Theatre-style arrangements work only for one-way information-giving, which is not the purpose of business meetings.

Create a clear objective for each meeting, but ensure that you don't try to deal with too many. How many are "too many"? More than one. Overloading the agenda just leads to frustration for all.

Communicate the agenda well in advance, accompanied by specific requests for preparation by all parties prior to the event. Attach readings, spreadsheets, etc. to allow participants to prepare themselves for discussion, debate, and decision.

LEAD THE MEETING WELL
Use the following skills to lead the discussion:

Clarify the meeting's intent. At the outset, clarify the objectives and agenda of the meeting, your role in it, their role in it, and logistics details. If this group is meeting for the first time, engage them in creating the communication ground rules that everyone will follow during this and all subsequent meetings. Avoid agenda creep by tabling non-relevant issues until another time.

Be enthusiastic, committed, respectful, and empathic. Nothing destroys the interest of the participants more than a disinterested leader or facilitator. Show interest, energy, enthusiasm, and commitment to the group through your verbal and nonverbal behavior and through the thoroughness of your preparation. Be respectful of participants' time, opinions, and ideas. Show empathy by arranging the meeting's logistics and agenda to appeal to the participants, who are, after all, your guests.

Encourage all to communicate openly. If anyone is unclear about the issue being discussed, the point being made, or the logic of the argument, encourage all to ask questions but in an open, honest, and tactful fashion.

Create a climate where—

♦ people talk candidly, openly, without threat of repercussion and where they listen actively to one another, not interrupting, over-interpreting, or finishing others' sentences for them
♦ the mutual intent is to learn rather than to defend or attack
♦ dialogue can occur: the free give and take of ideas to open up people's perspectives to allow for better decision making

Discourage debating and defending tactics. Instead of encouraging the playing of "Devil's Advocate" (often, just a superficial veil for personal attacks), encourage all members to play "Angel's Advocate," that is, to build on one another's ideas. Disagreement is normal in human communications. Draw it out and use it to sharpen different perspectives regarding the situation. Ask for examples, supporting evidence, contrasting ideas, etc.

Monitor the group. Encourage fairly equal participation among members. Encourage the less-assertive by directly asking for their opinions. Discourage dominators, either by discussing the issue with them privately or by structuring the group process to limit their contributions. Do the latter by having members write out their opinions regarding an issue before discussing them, ensuring that each person has the opportunity to speak. In a very aggressive group, use the "talking-stick" approach in which no one can speak unless he or she is holding the one "talking stick" possessed by the group. Be careful as facilitator, however, to discourage overly long examples or irrelevant discussion.

Provide paraphrased summaries of the meeting's progress. Occasionally summarize the discussion and restate it to the group to ensure that everyone is on the same page.

Juggle well. Your job as meeting leader is to juggle three balls without dropping any: time, the meeting's objectives, and member participation. If portions of the agenda take longer than expected, remind the group of deadlines and time allotments so the discussion can be shortened, the decision postponed, or the matter tabled.

Close well. Learn to tell when no additional value is being added through more discussion. Summarize to close the dialogue and decide the issue.

KEY 16

Present as a pro

Leaders help move others toward accomplishing desired objectives by making courageous decisions—regarding strategy, resources, operations, and distribution. They convey those decisions and create the motivational climate needed to implement them through persuasive communications. At the heart of this task are oral presentations—the most public of all communication acts.

Many leaders dread oral presentations. How do you develop rapport with your audiences? What are some of the most important keys to presenting yourself and your ideas well?

BUILDING RAPPORT

Like all other communications, preparation is the key to your success. But in addition to knowing what you want to say, you need to prepare well for your audience's acceptance of your message. Before you address any group, assess them carefully. Know their roles, job functions, values, aspirations, fears, goals, opinions, interest levels, motives, attitudes, probable questions, and probable objections.

Also, be sensitive to what audiences typically like and dislike.

Audiences usually like—

- ◆ Simple language. Don't use words strange to you and to them. Use words that paint a picture for the audience—in their language. Seek to create understanding, not to impress others.
- ◆ Simple phrases. Use concise sentences, frequent pauses, and rests. The audience likes to absorb one idea at a time. Simplicity is your guide.
- ◆ A presenter who knows his stuff. Don't attempt to bluff or present unfamiliar material unless you've done enough research. Ensure that you have done your homework, that you have the facts at your fingertips.
- ◆ A presenter who sticks to the time frame. Complete your talk in the time allowed. Keep your promises with the chair and the audience.
- ◆ Sincerity. Communicate your credentials but don't over-emphasize them. Be authentic, credible. The audience will spot a phony a mile away.
- ◆ Enthusiasm! Let yourself go. No one has ever been criticized for sincerely showing her passion about a subject. Dig in and give them the deal from the heart.

Audiences tend to dislike—

- ◆ A presenter who spends too much time getting started.

- One who has too much material for the time allowed.
- A presentation that has too many points or too much detail.
- A speaker with a displeasing voice—husky or harsh, monotonous, too low, stuttering, stumbling, indistinct, slurring, hesitant.
- A speaker with an attitude—condescending, arrogant, insulting, sarcastic, foul-mouthed, full of one's self.

PRESENTING YOURSELF WELL

Get your act together. First, get yourself kick-started, psyched-up, and pumped up. Your initial attitudes and behavior will set the tone, the note that will resonate throughout the presentation. Be totally prepared. Get to the presentation site early. Walk the room long before the first participant arrives. Ensure that everything (PowerPoint, flip charts, etc.) is ready to go. Focus, visualize a successful event, and dedicate yourself to providing the best presentation you have ever made—no matter if this is the first or the fifteenth time you have presented on that topic. Focus not on yourself but on your audience and purpose—to help move others in concert toward achieving the organization's vision. Go big, or stay home!

Greet your audience. If the group is a reasonable size, introduce yourself to audience members as they enter with a warm handshake and a sincere welcome. Get them comfortable. Make some small talk to lower the tension always there at the beginning of a presentation.

Make a good first impression. Dress and behave in ways that meet or exceed the audience's expectations of you. Introduce yourself. Establish your credentials, communicate your ethos (your values and guiding principles), and convey an upbeat, enthusiastic attitude toward the audience, the subject matter, and the occasion. Be sincere, honest, direct, compelling, engaging. Stand tall, with your weight evenly distributed; don't slouch; don't stand with most of your weight on one leg—or lean on the podium for support. Make good eye contact individually with each person in your audience, show some facial animation, and use some natural movement to emphasize your points.

Provide a short overview. Clearly convey the purposes of the presentation and how the content will help the audience. Clarify the agenda (sequence, timing, breaks, etc.).

Set the right climate. Here, for example, are some statements that help set a receptive climate:

◆ "I want to help make this presentation on _____ the most informative you have ever had on the topic."
◆ "Please ask questions as you have them."
◆ "I don't have all the answers but I have a few that you may find helpful."
◆ "I'm here to help you."

Get the audience comfortable and involved. Convince them that they will be active rather than passive during the presentation and that you will treat them as adults rather than as adolescents or children. Thus, use methods to get people participating right away, thinking and talking about your subject matter. Here are some possibilities:

◆ Engage members of the audience to identify on paper the questions that they would like addressed.
◆ Use a buzz group to get participants thinking and talking about the question or issue central to your presentation.

- Ask a rhetorical question; e.g., "Is this the time to plant or harvest?"
- Ask for a show of hands to a question; e.g., "How many of you would like to see a decrease in the amount of rework that we have been having to do?"

Structure your presentation well by offering a single unified theme through a clear opening, body, and close. Organize your main points into a logical pattern. Patterns to persuade, motivate, or inspire include problem/solution, cause and effect, theory/plan of action, listings (three reasons why we cannot lose the Dennison contract), costs/benefits, advantages/disadvantages, etc.

Encourage audience understanding. Convey information in digestible amounts at a suitable level and in a clear language. Explain and interpret the material; don't just present it. Identify key points by highlighting, repeating, and emphasizing them. Illustrate points through visual aids, examples, analogies, demonstrations, or hands-on activities. Encourage and respond to feedback by checking comprehension.

Enliven the presentation. Don't read your presentation. Use notes only. Use visuals, colorful anecdotes, sensory language, variation in voice, body language, and movement. Use gestures as long as they are motivated by an inner impulse and they don't draw undue attention to themselves.

Handle questions well:

- Make eye contact with the questioner. Ensure you understand the question. If not, continue questioning until you are clear.
- If clear, repeat the question so everyone can hear it.

- Answer the question, but don't make your response too long.
- After you answer, seek feedback from the questioner. Ask, "Is that clear?" or "Does that answer it?"
- When you don't know the answer, admit it. Say you aren't sure how to respond, and either say you will find the answer or defer the question to the audience for response.
- When a question and/or the questioner is hostile—pause before responding—take another breath—and don't jump to grab the bait. Encourage the person to expound, to "dump the emotional bucket." Paraphrase back what you're hearing—both the question and the emotions of the questioner. Show some empathy. Respond in a straightforward way. Do not lose emotional control no matter how difficult.

Close your presentation well. End it; don't just stop talking. Give your audience a sense of wholeness by referring back to your opening theme, providing a succinct summary, and ending with a call for action or a sincere expression of good will. As gymnasts do, "Stick the dismount."

KEY 17

Lead through active listening

O f all the communication requirements of an effective leader—conducting effective meetings, making powerful oral presentations, clarifying direction, giving feedback—nothing is more important than that of effective listening. Yet for many leaders, nothing is more difficult than learning to listen well. It requires unnatural patience, an unaccustomed attitude, and skills that are out of character for the typical top executive.

First, patience.

Many leaders—because they can size up people and situations quickly, desire action, and are driven toward achievement—are lousy listeners. They show it to others by finishing other people's sentences for them; doodling, tapping a pen, or shuffling papers when supposedly listening. They interrupt the speaker, allow themselves to be distracted by the telephone ringing, or show irritation if the conversation might require more than a minute or two. Most importantly, leaders often cannot stop talking.

There's the first tip: shut up. You cannot listen if you are talking. Nature gave us two ears but only one tongue—a gentle hint that we should listen twice as much as we talk!

Shut the door, hold all calls, and shut out other distractions, especially those in your head. Move from where you normally conduct business—a desk full of fires that need dousing—to a more peaceful spot, say a picnic table outside, the couch, anywhere that allows you to reduce distractions. Ensure that you have allocated enough time for the conversation.

Focus yourself and put yourself at ease. Take several deep breaths before your listening session, and visualize the positive results you wish to occur as a consequence. Just as you plan out what you are going to say, you need to do the same when listening. Write out questions you would like answered during the session.

Second, convey a positive attitude regarding listening and be highly motivated to listen well.

Put the speaker at ease by a firm handshake, open eye contact, and a friendly greeting. Authentically convey that you have been looking forward to listening. Invite your visitor to a beverage and a comfortable chair. Help her feel that she is free to talk through statements like: "There's no such thing as a dumb comment," "Please be honest, here," "You may speak in confidence to me." Reduce physical barriers between yourself and the other.

Show him that you are interested in understanding his point of view. Do not read your e-mail. Instead of opposing the speaker's perspective and judging her statements, put yourself in her place, and try to see the issue from her perspective. That is the purpose of listening: to enlarge and enrich your frame of reference regarding the world by seeing through another's frame of reference. As Stephen Covey's says in *The Seven Habits of Highly Effective People*, "Seek first to understand the other before you try to make yourself understood."

Keep calm; maintain your cool; don't lose your temper; don't make your reactions a barrier to understanding. Don't read more into what the person is saying than she intends.

Go easy on argument and criticism. Build on what your visitor is saying. Debating causes defensiveness, anger, or clamming up. Do not argue: even if you "win," you "lose." Before pointing out differences, state where you agree with the other person's position.

Use unnatural skills.

In addition to being calm under pressure, communicating deep interest, and showing low antagonism and judgment regarding the other person's views, a leader needs to develop skill in asking the appropriate questions and responding with appropriate feedback.

Ask the right questions to clarify the meaning of the other person's statements and to draw him out. In a calm, interested tone, ask open-ended questions that cannot be answered with a word or phrase. Use the initial responses as the basis of probing for more information, more explanation, more detail. Such response shows the talker that you are listening.

Encourage your visitor to expand what she said. Ask about her central idea or about nonverbal cues given off. Sometimes, use silence to encourage the other person to expand his statements. Use the simple expression, "Please tell me more."

Instead of ignoring or judging, reflect what you hear the other person saying—that is, restate as exactly as possible what she has said through words and nonverbals. Reflect out loud only sparingly, for overuse will make you appear sarcastic, rude, or stupid. But reflect silently all the time. That will help you use up mental capacity without judging the other before he or she has had a chance to complete the message.

Instead of challenging, paraphrase the important element of the speaker's lengthy or complex statement in your own words. Each of us has a different meaning for every noun, verb, adjective, and adverb in the English language. We also do not share the same interpretation of nonverbal cues. Share your understanding by phrasing interpretations tentatively so as to elicit additional feedback. "I'm hearing you're saying that we need to focus more on strategy rather than operations and that our lack of focus on the future is frustrating you. Am I interpreting you correctly?"

Reflecting and paraphrasing—difficult but learnable and doable skills—communicate acceptance and understanding.

Communication requires not only effective sending; it also requires engaging, effective, active listening.

KEY 18

Be conscious of nonverbal communications

When you are a leader, others interpret meaning in your every gesture, glance, and tone of voice. Thus, you must be critically conscious of your nonverbal communications—the messages you send through your body, face, tone of voice, and personal distance. A wink, a touch, or a grimace conveys vast meaning. When two people are communicating face to face, some 80 or 90 percent of the meaning is expressed nonverbally. Since nonverbal cues typically occur more spontaneously and are less consciously controlled than words, those who are receiving them read them as more accurate than verbal statements. So, when words and gestures contradict, nonverbal communications tend to be given most weight.

Here, because of length restrictions, we will discuss only American-style nonverbal communications. For treatment of international nonverbals, see Key 21.

Nonverbal communications take various forms:

Reproof on her lips, but a smile in her eye.

Samuel Lover

paralanguage, gestures, facial expressions, eye contact, posture, touch, dress, and proxemics. The following discussion is based in part on *Business Communication: A Technology Based Approach*, by W. P. Galle, Jr., B. H. Nelson, D. W. Luse, and M. F. Valliere (Chicago, Irwin, 1996, pp. 534–535).

Paralanguage concerns how something is said, including all vocal aspects of speech other than words. Voice qualities—such as pitch, rhythm, tempo, and volume—influence how others interpret your words. A soft, low-pitched voice and slow rate indicate liking; a high-pitched voice communicates anger. A monotone indicates boredom. Vocal characterizers—coughing, yawning, grunting—can sometimes be used effectively, but because they distract and annoy, it is best to avoid them. Vocal qualifiers—variations in tone or intensity—communicate a lot. For example, increases in rate or volume may indicate impatience, excitement, or anger. See the power of verbal qualifiers by repeating the sentence, "I didn't say he stole your car," seven times, stressing a different word each time. Finally—vocal segregates—pauses such as "ah" and "um"—may suggest lack of confidence and organization.

Some gestures, like a thumbs-up, have specific meanings understood in a particular culture or occupation. Others, such as self-stroking, are interpreted as anxiousness, guilt, or suspicion.

One's face can form 250,000 different expressions, most of which convey emotions—joy, sadness, anger, fear, surprise, and disgust. Even when people try to suppress facial expressions, they still send them, lasting but a fraction of a second, revealing their feelings.

Eye contact, the most telling of all nonverbal communications, tends to regulate conversation. Open eye contact suggests understanding, interest, and inclusion. Seeking eye contact communicates one's desire to converse; avoiding eye contact conveys the opposite. Also, glaring or staring conveys intimidation or distrust.

Posture, or body positioning, conveys especially openness, confidence, and interest and their opposites. For example, if a customer relaxes her arms and leans forward as she talks to a sales clerk, her posture reflects approval and acceptance of the other's message. If she leans back, arms crossed, her posture suggests rejection or disagreement.

Touch can convey warmth, understanding, and intimacy. For example, research shows when a clerk lightly touches a customer on the arm, the customer sees the person more positively, views the situation more positively, and is more likely to comply. Note, though, this research involved casual touching. Many other forms of touch may be resented; unwanted touching can be a form of sexual harassment.

When we meet another, we probably notice first the way he or she is dressed. Dress can convey self-image, mood, identity, power, wealth, or authority. People dressed formally are better able to command respect.

Proxemics, the use of distance, conveys status or degree of intimacy. Sitting at the head of a table conveys status; standing close to another, intimacy; and sitting behind a desk (as opposed to alongside it), a superior-subordinate relationship. Two elements—personal space and seating arrangements—are especially relevant.

◆ Personal space is your self-established area of privacy. The personal zone, from about eighteen inches to four feet, is used for comfortable interaction with others and connotes closeness and friendship. The social zone, from 4 to 12 feet, is used for most business. People collaborating use the inner part of this zone; the outer part is used for more formal interactions. Typically, a person feels uncomfortable when his personal space is violated. He will generally protest or leave the situation rather than accept it.

◆ Where one sits is also important. Leaders often choose positions of potentially high eye contact with others, such as the front of a room or the head of a table. A person randomly placed there is more likely to be perceived as a leader than a person placed elsewhere. Communications flow her way, and she is likely to be perceived as having high status. Further, if individuals are allowed to seat themselves around a table, they tend to choose arrangements appropriate for the task. When people expect to be cooperating, they sit side by side. When they expect to compete, they tend to sit face to face.

KEY 19

Manage conflict

Because you are often the hub of organizational communications—in the "middle of things"—as leader you must regularly deal with conflict. Some conflict occurs because people have truly different perspectives regarding vision, decisions, resource allocation, and the like. But many more conflicts result from simply not understanding the other person's perspective. Instead of running away from conflict (withdrawing or avoiding) or trying to fight for your position, learn to manage conflicts by adopting an "intent to learn" rather than an intent to protect. Try to create and sustain relationships marked by what Stephen Covey calls "win-win, or no deal."

Here's some enlightened common sense about conflict and some tips regarding how to help resolve differences:

Conflict and disagreement are normal in human relationships. Because of different life experiences (upbringing, culture, education, previous experience in relationships, etc.), people inevitably see the world differently. Most think that their view is the "correct" one, for we interpret the world though our own limited experience.

People are often in conflict because they do not understand the other person's frame of reference; do not understand or share the same values, objectives, and priorities; or are competing for the same resources—attention, money, position, etc.—and believe there's not enough to go around.

Conflict is good. Conflict provides an opportunity for people to recognize and value differences of opinion, open up their worldview, expand their perspective, and solve problems. It gives both parties the opportunity to learn, to improve, to practice tolerance, and to achieve satisfactory resolution of emotional tension that often hampers both parties' creativity, productivity, trust, and communications both on and off the job.

A mutually acceptable solution can often be found. If one can adopt an abundance mentality and communicate in an honest but considerate and respectful manner, people can move from disagreement to compromise to collaboration to synergy.

Any of the parties in conflict can contribute to its resolution if one takes personal responsibility and initiates communications. Consider the following:

◆ Your contribution to relationships is under your control; the part others choose to play is not under your control.
◆ When you change, your relationships change.
◆ Waiting for other persons or situations to change so that you can change equals no change.

- The way you are treated by others depends partly upon how you "train" them to treat you.
- Risk-taking is part of conflict management. You may be rejected.

Trusting behavior can evoke trusting behavior. The principle of social reciprocity stipulates that you get back what you give to others. "What goes around, comes around." If you want others to trust you, listen to you, care for you, respect you, etc., you must give it first. You then stand a better chance of having it returned. You demonstrate trusting behavior by empowering others, being open to influence, taking some risks, and being willing to change when faced with new information. As Sitting Bull once said, "Offer your opponent the peace pipe first."

Consensus and synergy are likely only when people choose to cooperate in a win-win relationship rather than compete. Sometimes you must accommodate; other times, you must compete with all you have. Because of past experiences (often deprivations, rejections, and other painful emotional experiences), some people cannot *not* try to compete, to win at all costs, even at the expense of personal relationships. When dealing with a battler on an unimportant issue, let him win so you can gather social credits for later use. When dealing with a critical issue, as Sitting Bull continued, "Fight them with everything you have. And when it is over, let bygones be bygones."

Some conflicts may never be resolved because of fear, rigidity, intolerance, anger, paranoia, or other emotional impairment. Most often it is best to sidestep others' negativity, sarcasm, and malicious ridicule. Often, people with low self-esteem ridicule others so they can feel better about themselves. Rather than taking such stuff personally, be assertive and be honest regarding your convictions and your rights to be treated with respect.

HOW TO COMMUNICATE IN CONFLICT SITUATIONS

Come to agreement with your conflicting party to follow these guidelines to build more positive, less stressful, and more productive relationships. Above all, both parties need to approach this communication with an intent to learn rather than an intent to protect.

- ◆ Be honest; say what's on your mind now. Be open.
- ◆ Be specific; provide examples.
- ◆ Don't use the words "never" and "always."
- ◆ Listen in depth; reflect and paraphrase what you hear.
- ◆ Ask questions to clarify the meaning of what the other person is saying.
- ◆ Focus on behavior that the other person controls.
- ◆ Maintain good eye contact.
- ◆ Focus on only one specific issue or behavior at a time.
- ◆ Don't interrupt.
- ◆ Stay there. Don't walk away mentally, emotionally, physically, or psychologically.
- ◆ Be direct but tactful.
- ◆ Use "I" statements rather than "You" statements; e.g., "When this happens, I feel . . ." rather than "When you do this, it makes me feel. . . ."
- ◆ Don't attack the other person by ridiculing, taunting, or otherwise being rude and hostile.
- ◆ Don't defend yourself by blaming others, avoiding, and withdrawing.

KEY 20

Manage organizational culture

O rganizational culture consists of the values, symbols, stories, heroes, and rites that have special meaning for a company's people. Culture represents the emotional, intangible part of the organization. If structure is the organization's skeleton, culture is its soul.

Companies like Southwest Airlines, Quad-Graphics, Nordstrom, Disney, and General Electric credit their distinctive cultures for much of their success. Of 400 CEOs in North America and Europe interviewed by Price Waterhouse, 47 percent said that reshaping culture and related employee behavior took up a great deal of their time and was as important as monitoring financial information.

It is relatively easy to document a new machine's costs and benefits. You can also demonstrate the short-term savings of slashing the workforce. Because these things can be measured, we tend to focus on them.

But what are the true costs of a reorganization that leaves workers overburdened, angry, and stressed? What are the hidden costs of a merger that, while attractive "on paper," leads to internal clashes over core values and assumptions about "the right way to do things"? Conversely, what would be the benefits of a culture that instills values of cooperation and creativity, that fosters loyalty, and that is seen as a "great place to be"? Because these things are difficult to measure, we tend to ignore them. Culture, though, is real, and it is important. A recent study of 200 mergers found incompatible cultures to be the primary cause of failures.

If something is to provide competitive advantage for a firm, it must be valuable, rare, and difficult to imitate. Unlike new technology, a pricing strategy, or a product design, an organizational culture is unique and impossible to duplicate. As such, it has the potential to yield great and enduring strategic advantage. But a strong culture can be destroyed overnight through an ill-advised redesign, an ill-planned merger, or a rash downsizing.

As a leader, you are a creator, shaper, guardian, and communicator of organizational culture. You play these roles through the behaviors you model, the things you expect and reward, the policies you set, the messages you send, and the cultural elements you employ. Let's consider five key elements of organizational culture:

Values are the things that are important in an organization. They are deep-seated, personal standards that influence our moral judgments, responses to others, and commitment to personal and organizational goals. Values, the bedrock of organizational culture, let employees know how they are expected to behave and what actions are acceptable. The sharing of values is key to the development of a successful organizational culture.

At Hewlett-Packard, a clear focus on the five values of the "HP Way"—We have trust and respect for individuals. We focus on a high level of achievement and contribution. We conduct our business with uncompromising integrity. We achieve our common objectives through teamwork. We encourage flexibility and innovation.— gives HP a competitive edge in the global environment.

Symbols are things that stand for or suggest something else. Office assignments signal status. Dress codes suggest the level of formality. A logo can influence customer and employee perceptions. Mary Kay Ash chose the Mary Kay Cosmetics Bumblebee as a symbol for her organization because, "Aerodynamically the bumblebee shouldn't be able to fly, but the bumblebee doesn't know that so it goes on flying anyway." And, an action can be symbolic. Consider the "Lambeau Leap" where a Green Bay Packers player leaps into the arms of hometown fans in the stands at Lambeau Field after scoring a touchdown, symbolizing oneness with the Green Bay faithful.

Narratives are written or spoken accounts used by members of the organization to make sense of their experiences and express their feelings and beliefs. Narratives often reflect basic themes— whether, for example, the organizational culture supports equality or inequality, security or insecurity, and control or lack of control. A story widely repeated at IBM tells of how Tom Watson praised a security guard who required him to go back for his identification. A similar story is told at Revlon, differing in just one detail: when a Revlon receptionist refused to let Charles Revson walk off with a sign-in sheet, he fired her. The first story conveys a sense of egalitarianism, saying, "We all obey the rules." The second conveys the opposite, saying, "We obey the rulers."

Heroes are company role models. In their actions, character, and support of the existing organizational culture, they highlight the values a company wishes to reinforce. Heroes are often the main characters of organizational narratives. CEOs like Herb Kelleher at Southwest Airlines, Anita Roddick at the Body Shop, and Jack Welch at GE are heroes in their firms. But, heroes may come from all levels, such as an employee who persevered to champion an important new product or who provided extraordinary effort when the company faced a crisis.

Rites combine cultural forms into a public performance. Rites of passage mark important transitions. For instance, employees who complete a rigorous management training program offsite may be welcomed back with a speech, certificate, and perhaps a cocktail party. Rites of enhancement celebrate accomplishments of members, enhancing their status. For example, Mary Kay Cosmetics is famous for the diamond pins, furs, and pink Cadillacs awarded to its top performers at elaborate meetings called Mary Kay Seminars. Participants, dressed in fancy evening clothes, receive their awards on the stage of an auditorium, to the cheers of a large audience. Rites of integration bring people together to revive shared feelings that bind and commit them to the organization. An annual holiday party is a rite of integration. So is the Wal-Mart annual meeting, where 20,000 shareholders come together to see featured celebrities, hear inspiring stories, watch videos about Wal-Mart's accomplishments, and join in the Wal-Mart cheer. And, so are the "meetings" of Harley-Davidson's H.O.G. (Harley Owners Group) chapters, where "the bond is metal" as hundreds of Harley riders hit the road together to help out worthy causes or just "share the awareness."

Some organizational cultures are "stronger" than others. In strong cultures members agree on important values and hold them with passion. Strong cultures encourage cooperation, improve communication, and enhance commitment. To build a strong culture, a leader must take culture seriously.

You say you don't have the time? Jack Welch, CEO of General Electric, has gone to Crotonville, GE's Leadership Development Center, every two weeks for more than 15 years to run leadership training programs, teach the GE Management Values statement, and reinforce the GE culture. Jack Welch finds the time.

KEY 21

Get ready for globalization

With globalization, the world's people are becoming more interconnected with respect to the cultural, political, technological, and environmental aspects of their lives. What does this mean for you?

You are likely to spend at least part of your career in other countries. In fact, some companies now require international experience for their top managers.

According to Andrew Grove, Chairman of Intel, with globalization "every employee will compete with every person in the world who is capable of doing the same job. There are a lot of them, and many of them are very hungry."

You may suddenly find yourself working for a foreign firm. International mergers and acquisitions reached an all-time high of $544.31 billion in 1998. While U.S. companies have historically been the world's biggest buyers, United Kingdom firms have now taken over the lead. Increasingly, you may be working for a firm headquartered in Germany, Sweden, Japan, or almost anywhere else in the world.

Your firm—and your job—will increasingly depend on international trade. Directly or indirectly, international trade now accounts for about 20 percent of all jobs in the U.S.

You will be managing a diverse workforce even if you never leave the U.S. Consider that Asians, Hispanics, African-Americans, and other nonwhite groups are projected to make up 47 percent of the U.S. population by the year 2050. The Hispanic population is projected to grow from 24 million (9 percent of the population) to 81 million (21 percent). The number of Asian-Americans is expected to jump from 7 million to 35 million by 2040. The diversity provided by these groups is even greater than a listing of categories such as "Asian-American" and "Hispanic" might suggest. For example, Hispanics represent different races and many nationalities, including Mexicans, Cubans, Puerto Ricans, Spanish, Dominican Republicans, and people from 15 other Central and South American countries, all with different histories, labor force characteristics, and growth rates.

So, whether you are leading in Lima, Ohio or Lima, Peru, you will be managing a diverse workforce, dealing with global competitors, or even working for a foreign firm. What should you expect as you deal with people from other national cultures? Geert Hofstede, a Dutch researcher who worked as a psychologist for IBM, studied 116,000 people working in sixty-four countries and identified five important dimensions where national cultures differ:

Individualism versus collectivism. In individualistic

cultures, such as the United States and Australia, the cultural belief is that the individual comes first— social frameworks are loosely knit and people are chiefly expected to look after their own interests and those of their immediate family. There is an emphasis on individual achievement. Society offers individuals a great amount of freedom and people are used to making independent decisions and taking independent action. In collectivist cultures, such as Japan and Pakistan, there are tight social frameworks in which people expect to be looked after within their groups and protected by the group in times of trouble. In exchange for security, loyalty is expected.

Power distance is the degree to which a society accepts the fact that power in institutions and organizations is distributed unequally. A high-power-distance society—the Philippines, Mexico, or India, for example—accepts wide differences in power in organizations. Employees show great respect for authority, titles, status, and rank. Titles are important in bargaining. A low-power-distance society—Denmark, Israel, and Ireland stand out— plays down inequalities as much as possible.

Uncertainty avoidance refers to the way societies deal with risk and uncertainty. In low-uncertainty-avoidance countries, such as Switzerland and Denmark, people are relatively comfortable with risks and tolerate behaviors and opinions that differ from their own. In high-uncertainty-avoidance countries, such as Portugal and Greece, formal rules and other mechanisms are used to provide security and reduce risk. There is less tolerance for deviant ideas and behaviors.

Quality versus quantity of life. Some cultures, like Japan and Venezuela, emphasize the quantity of life and value assertiveness and the acquisition of money and material things. Other cultures, such as the Scandinavian countries, emphasize the quality of life and show greater sensitivity and concern for the welfare of others.

Time orientation. Citizens of some countries, such as Japan and China, have a long-term orientation, deriving from values that include thrift (saving) and persistence in achieving goals. Those of other countries, such as France and Indonesia, have a short-term orientation, deriving from values that express a concern for maintaining personal stability or happiness and living for the present.

Another key factor is whether cultures are high or low context. In a high-context culture, such as most Asian, Hispanic, African, and Arab countries, the context in which a communication occurs is just as important as the words that are actually spoken, and cultural clues are important in understanding what is being communicated. The context includes the social setting, use of phrasing, gestures and tone of voice, and the person's history and status. In a low-context culture, such as Germany or the United States, the words used by the speaker much more explicitly convey the speaker's message to the listener. This suggests that nonverbal communications, while important in all settings, are especially critical in high-context cultures. Most immigrants to the U.S. are now coming from high-context cultures.

Nonverbal communications have dramatically different meanings across cultures. Roger Axtell, in his books *Gestures* and *Do's and Taboos Around the World*, provides fascinating examples of these differences. For instance, nodding your head means "Yes" in most countries but "No" in Bulgaria and Greece. The classic "OK" sign of thumb and forefinger forming a circle can imply "money" in Japan, means "worthless" in France, and is considered an obscene gesture in Brazil, Germany, and Russia. In

Saudi Arabia, to cross your legs in such a way that you display the sole of your foot to your host is a grievous affront. While North Americans often wave to signal "Hello" or "Goodbye," this action signals "No!" in much of Europe.

There are also cultural differences in the meaning of eye contact. While Americans generally expect eye contact in a conversation, many Asians and Hispanics consider eye contact, especially with a superior, to be utterly disrespectful. In countries like Libya, looking a woman in the eye for more than a short time is considered a form of assault.

Appropriate interpersonal distances also vary by culture. For example, "cool cultures"—like those in Northern Europe and the United States—require more personal space, while "warm cultures," including India, the Caribbean, and the Middle East, require less space. In the Middle East, it is the custom for business associates to embrace each other and to kiss lightly on the cheek, and the space between business associates is only about a foot. A business executive entering another culture must be especially careful to learn appropriate zones for various interactions. So:

◆ Recognize that you will be leading in a global environment—this is not an option. Get ready for it.
◆ Be sensitive to cultural differences. If you will be dealing with individuals from other national cultures, do your homework.
◆ Above all else, remember that your perceptions, attitudes, and behaviors have been shaped by your own culture, just as those of members of other societies have been shaped by theirs. You will get farther in the global environment by seeking understanding than by judging.

KEY 22

Initiate change well

A s Harvard Professor John Kotter points out, a leader functions "to move a group or individual in directions that ultimately are in the long-term best interests of all stakeholders." Jim Kouzes and Barry Posner state that "Challenging the Process" is the first of all leadership practices.

"Leaders—

1. Search out challenging opportunities to change, grow, innovate, and improve.

2. Experiment, take risks, and learn from the accompanying mistakes."

Leaders make change happen, initiate improvements, make the world different. Most people tend to seek pleasure and avoid pain. But almost all change involves disruption of safe, comfortable routines. That's why leaders meet resistance.

What can leaders do to reduce human inertia, and

encourage participation, cooperation, or, at least compliance?

Aristotle argued that all attempts to encourage others to change their minds, feelings, and behavior can be summarized as follows:

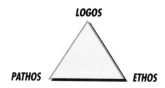

Here, *logos* refers to convincing another person to accept a change through reason, logic, and data; *ethos*, through the strength of your moral character and the trust that followers have in you; and *pathos*, through appeals to your target audience's emotional and psychological needs.

Logos
When people are told about a change at work that will affect them, they normally react by first asking "Why?" When you initiate change, then, be prepared to provide a clear rationale in a direct, well-supported manner, using education and communication as your persuasive method. Ensure that your proposed change meets at least one of these tests to be worth the disruption it may cause:

- ◆ Will the change enhance productivity, improve quality, or reduce costs?
- ◆ Will it provide customers with greater value?
- ◆ Will it help keep the organization up to date with technology?
- ◆ Will it help us grow and develop?

Do your homework, gathering relevant facts that prove a real problem exists. Identify potential causes and pinpoint probable causes. Thoroughly describe on paper the problem or opportunity, its causes, the need to do something about it, alternative solutions, and the cost-benefit of each. Communicate clearly the advantages and disadvantages of the change you are selling.

Identify sources of help. Who could help you sell the change? Staff, managers, inside/outside experts?

Anticipate questions and objections. Think about the change from others' points of view. Identify the questions you would have and the objections you would raise if you were the target of this change.

Sell the benefits of the change in terms of the perspective of those who will have to go through it. How will the change help make things better and avoid or reduce bad consequences?

Listen in depth to their concerns, questions, and fears.

Create an implementation plan that answers the key questions most people have when faced with change: who, what, where, when, why, and how.

ETHOS
People tend to cooperate with a leader who has high credibility, a combination of competence and trustworthiness.

People tend to believe someone who demonstrates expertise and authoritativeness, has the requisite qualifications, and comes across to them as experienced, informed, skilled, and intelligent. When faced with a persuasive argument, the audience asks, "Does this person know the truth?"

The other dimension is trustworthiness: one's

Change is not made without inconvenience, even from worse to better.

Richard Hooker

character, moral fiber, and personal integrity. When faced with a persuasive argument, the audience asks, "Does this person tell the truth?"

PATHOS

You may have a rational idea for change, one that has a great cost-benefit ratio. You also may be seen as a trusted person of strong moral character and technical competence. That's not enough to persuade people to change, however. You also must attend to your target audience's emotional and psychological needs.

If the change you are initiating threatens people's emotional safety and security—if it lowers their self-confidence or self-esteem—you may get begrudging compliance or none at all. One effective way to satisfy people's emotional needs and stimulate high motivation is to get them actively involved in the change itself. When people feel like they have had a voice and a hand in shaping the change and its implementation, they tend to adopt ownership of it. Now, it isn't just you; "I has turned to We." Such participation and involvement can be sought at stages in the process or throughout, depending on the competence of the players.

Using participation in planning and implementing changes simultaneously enriches people's work, raises self-esteem and self-confidence, and hones their problem-solving skills. In this way, you may turn what at first looks like win/lose into a win/win proposition for all.

Some changes, however—no matter how you try to sell them—create winners and losers. Productivity improvements, for example, sometimes result in unneeded staff. You initiate such painful change by providing facilitation and emotional support and by negotiating, compromising, and compensating the individuals for their loss. Here the leader pays special attention to people's emotional needs and concerns, and to their pocketbooks. Eliminating a job but transferring the person to a less-desirable but higher-paying job is an example. Providing a generous severance-pay package is another.

MANIPULATION AND COERCION

As leader, you can use other forms of persuasion—that of manipulating people through misinformation and downright lies, demanding change in a forceful, dictatorial manner, or threatening people with punishments if they fail to comply.

Do these tactics work? Yes, but usually at high costs to morale, to positive working relationships, willing cooperation, and your trustworthiness as a leader.

The best advice? Sit closer to Aristotle.

KEY 23

Define your organization's vision, mission, values, credo, goals, and strategy

Many organizations live from day to day, with no strategic direction to guide their members. True leaders—from Gandhi to Lee Iacocca to Mother Teresa—lead through strategic vision, have a clear mission, espouse strong core values, model specific behaviors, accomplish stretching goals, and formulate strategy to accomplish them.

Look in any book on leadership and strategy, and you will see a great deal of variability regarding definitions of these important terms. Because statements of vision and mission are critical to the leader and the organization, let's wade through the clutter of definitions to emerge with clear meanings. These statements will serve you and your organization well as tools to set and keep yourself and your organization's resources focused and deployed appropriately.

Vision: A vivid description of a person's or organization's preferred future. A vision can be simple or complex, concise or elaborate, but it must be clear, engaging, compelling, sincere, and stretching.

We are committed to becoming the primary, comprehensive, and convenient financial-services center for all its members, and a place where—

Everybody Counts: Every member, every employee, every contact
Everybody Cares: Show respect, project empathy, practice humility
Everybody Delivers: Excellence with pride and excitement
Every Day

—*University of Wisconsin Credit Union*

"To create a positive team environment which encourages and fosters personal growth, where employees feel great pride in accomplishing; high-quality, very friendly personal service; fabulous-looking stores; facilities and grounds that reflect great attention to detail; stores filled with extremely happy customers and employees; a reputation as the undisputed market leader; and dedication to community partnership."

—*American Television and Appliance*

"To be named MVP of the NFL and to lead the Green Bay Packers to victory in the Super Bowl."   —*Brett Favre, 1996*

"Blue water, pine trees, and, tomorrow, I help adults learn something significant."   —*Buck Joseph, 1979*

Mission: An organization's business focus and scope, the range of its products and services, the geographical range of its offerings, and its purpose. It answers these questions: "What business are we in?" "What is our niche?" "Who are our customers?" "Where do we operate?" "How do we deliver our products/services?" and, most importantly, "Why do we exist?"

Naval Credit Union, a member-owned cooperative, exists to provide our members with financial security. Through personal service, conveniently located branches, and up-to-date technology, we provide personal financial services to Argon Naval Air Station's enlisted personnel and officers, both in active service and retired, and their families. These services include mortgage loans, share-draft and savings accounts, VISA/Master Card services, and ATMs

Core Principles/Guiding Values: The central beliefs undergirding an organization's treatment of its external and internal stakeholders. These values or principles, which define the fundamental way it operates, usually number at least three. Some organizations list over 40 core values. Some use 10; others, just three to five.

Respect for the Individual.
Caring about the dignity and rights of each person in the organization, and not just when it is convenient or expedient to do so.

Customer Service.
Giving the best customer service of any company in the world. Not some of the time, but all the time.

Excellence.
Believing that all jobs and projects should be performed in a superior manner.   *—IBM*

- TELL THE TRUTH
- KEEP YOUR PROMISES
- BE FAIR
- RESPECT THE INDIVIDUAL
- ENCOURAGE INTELLECTUAL CURIOSITY
    —Harley-Davidson Motor Company

Credo of Behavior: The specific, often measurable behaviors that the organization pledges to demonstrate toward its external and internal stakeholders. The best Credo statements are usually concise, simple, clear, and concrete. They describe what people can see and hear.

Cleanliness, Service, Value, and Courtesy—*McDonald's*

- Simplify
- Use little paper
- Be professional
- Provide autonomy
- Keep no files
- Promote from within
- Involve everyone
- Decentralize
- Share the rewards

—*Nine of "Dana's Forty Thoughts," Dana Corporation*

Understand clients thoroughly, their firms, their products and services, their directions, their needs and wants.

Meet clients where they are; gear language and level of instruction to their needs.

Promise only what we can deliver; deliver what we promise.

Start on time, end on time, and don't waste the clients' time during an instructional event.

—*Four of thirty-seven of Management Institute's Credo, 1988*

Goals: The large but specific targets the organization desires to accomplish to enable the vision to be fulfilled.

"Before the decade is out, . . . landing a man on the moon and returning him safely to earth."

—*President John F. Kennedy, 1961*

"Double the number of stores and increase the dollar volume per square foot 60% by the year 2000."

—*Sam Walton, President and CEO, 1990*

"Beat Coke."   —*Pepsi*

Critical Strategic Imperatives: The critical actions the organization will undertake to accomplish the goals.

"Six-Sigma Quality (a defect rate not greater than 3.4 per million)
Total Cycle-Time Reduction
Product and Manufacturing Leadership
Profit Improvement
Participative Management within, and Cooperation between Organizations"

—Motorola

KEY 24

Use participation to create vision

Many people today demand a more participative style of leadership. They want a leader who not only involves them in creating the organization's goals and strategies but includes them into putting them into action. The commitment generated by sharing leadership glues the firm together and aligns it toward common goals. Participating as a member of the team that creates the organization's preferred future also adds to the motivation to help realize it. The greatest vision—unimplemented—adds no value.

Other stakeholders to involve may include your executive or management team, members of the Board of Directors, key staff, even customers. Such a team-developed vision guides shorter-term operational goals and action plans at lower levels of the organization. Here's some advice:

Carefully select team members. Choose only those who have lots to contribute because (a) they are sensitive to your business's environment, competition, and industry trends; and (b) they think strategically—"down-board," as a good chess player does. Do not select a person just because you like her, wish not to hurt someone, or want to co-opt someone.

Use a professional facilitator to work with the vision team, laying out and implementing a structured process to draft the vision. Why a facilitator? Without someone to keep the work moving, the group honest, and everyone participating, you may get just another committee. Robert Copeland once said, "To get something done, a committee should consist of no more than three people, two of whom are absent."

Answer these questions early:

◆ What is the vision's purpose? What are we trying to accomplish by creating one? What are we going to do with it? If you answer, "Well, everyone is doing it," resist the temptation. If you answer, "We need a clear direction for our organization during the next X years," you're right on.
◆ Who is the audience for the vision? Customers? Staff? Shareholders? Everyone?
◆ What elements should be included? Mission? Vision? Values? Credo of Behaviors? Big goals? Strategies?

Have each member perform a S.W.O.T. analysis regarding your organization and its competitive environment. S.W.O.T. stands for:

◆ Strengths: Current assets, strengths, and distinctive competencies of the organization
◆ Weaknesses: Current liabilities, weaknesses, and downsides

- Opportunities: Potential future opportunities that lie outside the organization in its markets, its customers' needs and wants, its regulatory environment, availability of capital, etc.
- Threats: Potential future threats to the organization from competitors, product obsolescence, changing customer's needs and wants, etc.

Meet as a group with your facilitator to discuss, debate, and develop consensus regarding the:

- most significant strengths you wish to maximize
- most important weaknesses you wish to strengthen or minimize
- best potential opportunities to explore
- worst threats you must deal with in the future

Use the consensus SWOT analysis and have each team member answer questions about the preferred future of your organization. (Take a week to answer. Assume it is now a date 2–5 years in the future):

- What is the organization doing that makes you happy, gives you satisfaction and bliss? What is it not doing now that used to give you pain and sorrow?
- What's improved in the business?
- Why has *INC.* magazine featured you as an example of an outstanding organization?
- What big goals have been accomplished? What challenges have been met?
- How are staff members treating one another? Treating customers?
- What are your competitors saying about you that really pleases you?

- What is the organization working on? How is it spending its resources in (fill in the year) that is different from how it spends them now?
- What numbers indicate that you are making great progress?
- What use are you making of what technology to enhance your business?
- What distinctive competitive advantage are you leveraging?

During the next team meeting, each member should walk the others though his responses. The facilitator drafts the salient points on flip charts, posts them, and helps the group identify commonalties and areas of contradiction. Commonalties are questioned, and differences used to sharpen members' assumptions about the organization's future. The facilitator then helps the group classify the data into the various forms mentioned earlier: mission, vision, values, credo, goals, and strategies.

Instead of trying to "word-smith" the initial draft of the vision as a team, have one member— someone with solid writing skills and a deep sense of the organization—boil the classified data into drafts of each element.

Meet two weeks later to discuss, amend, and approve the draft vision and its elements. Validate this draft by seeking feedback from a broader representation of stakeholders. Revise accordingly. Again, do not concern yourself with the specific words. Leave that to the writer.

Now that you have a solid vision statement, one that has encouraged fairly widespread participation and incorporated various inputs, you have a good start. You have taken a critical step, probably the biggest in leadership: shaping the preferred future of your organization. But be aware—you have just started.

KEY 25

Turn vision into reality

W hat does a leader do to turn vision into concrete reality? What's critical in communications and implementing?

COMMUNICATING THE VISION

Publish the final statement. Make it visible! But do so face-to-face. Leaders of the organization should distribute it and discuss with staff its meaning and implications. Ensure that all understand it and their role in fulfilling it. Distribute it in brochures and newsletters, on plaques and posters, on videotape. Print the credo of behavior or your statement of values on "Vision Cards," laminated and cut to the size of a credit card for employees to carry in their wallets for easy reference. Keep the vision in front of people.

Use elements of the statement in advertising and promotions. Communicate it in letters to staff, the board of directors, members of the community and governmental bodies. For example, Ford Motor Company's advertising program "Quality is

Job 1" was derived directly from the company's statement of guiding principles.

Incorporate the statement into employee handbooks, orientation sessions, and training programs. Don Percy, the former president of the University of Wisconsin Credit Union, the largest in the state, oriented each new employee to the organization by personally discussing at length the credit union's vision and core values.

Using the credo of behaviors as criteria, gather survey data from customers and employees to understand how well your organization is living up to its beliefs—Johnson & Johnson, for example, surveys its employees every year to determine the degree to which the credo is being lived out by each division. Give the data to staff and make appropriate changes.

Review the statements often and amend them. Do not make the process a one-time exercise.

Measure your organization's success in progressing toward fulfilling the vision.

Live it daily. Leaders must serve as role models of the "Vision in Action." Without visible action, the vision becomes progressively more abstract and, therefore, less powerful as a guide to behavior and decision making.

PLANNING FOR IMPLEMENTATION

Only after the vision document have been drafted and communicated to everyone affected by it does the critical process begin: planning for its implementation. Planning consists of (1) creating specific goals, strategies, and action plans; and (2) ensuring that your management system encourages staff to carry it out.

(1) Creating Specific Plans:
Decide which major business products and services are required to accomplish the vision and fulfill the mission.

For each of these products and services, establish criteria for success, and determine measures and performance targets for each year during the vision period:

Criteria for Success	Target (2000-2002)
Net Profit	12% per year
Revenue growth per square foot of floor space	> 15% but < 25% per year
Return on Assets	20% per year
Customer Satisfaction	95% of annual survey rate services as "good" or "excellent"
New Product Revenue	25% of revenue must come from products/ services introduced within last three years
Training and Development	20 hours of formal continuing education per year for each employee
Safety	Reduce and maintain lost-time due to injuries to 1997–1999 levels.
Leadership Succession	Identify, assess, and complete developmental activities for two high-potential candidates.

Compare current performance against your targeted performance. Identify strategies and resources required to close each gap.

Develop action steps under each strategy that stipulate in a year-by-year fashion what will be done, in what sequence, by whom, using what resources, and by what date. Ensure that the next fiscal year's action plan is clear, concrete, specific, but also plan a logical sequence of actions to ensure that the vision is fully implemented by your target date.

Coordinate the action plans to promote efficient and effective use of resources.

(2) Adjusting Your Management System:
As important as specific action plans are, no plan will be implemented well until the people who do the work are provided with the necessary support to perform. For people to live out plans, they need:

- ◆ Skills. Hire well-trained people, or ensure that workers get the needed training and development to carry out the plans.
- ◆ Resources. Ensure that tools, equipment, information, and facilities are in place.
- ◆ Accountability and responsibility. Communicate such critical matters through job descriptions, orientation sessions, and supervisory communications.
- ◆ Feedback. The best feedback is measurable, honest, specific, and visible.
- ◆ Rewards. Encourage people to stretch by providing both financial and non-financial incentives for improving performance.

As we complete this key we leave you to pursue your journey. We hope these keys will provide you with practical tools for that journey of leadership. It has been a pleasure outfitting you.

INDEX

AUTHORS

RAY ALDAG, Ph.D., is the Pyle Bascom Professor of Business Leadership, Chair of the Department of Management and Human Resources, and Co-Director of the Center for the Study of Organizational Performance in the Graduate School of Business at the University of Wisconsin. He has served on more than 50 P.h.D. thesis committees and has published more than 70 journal articles and book chapters. A past president of the National Academy of Management, he is the co-author of 5 books.

BUCK JOSEPH, Ed.D., is Associate Professor of Management and Director of Business Communications Programs for the Management Institute, The School of Business at the University of Wisconsin. He teaches Business Communications in the Executive MBA program of the School of Business and works regularly with companies throughout the nation, tailoring training programs at the executive, mid-management, and the first-line leader levels. Dr. Joseph conducts in-house training and development programs for such clients as 3M Corporation, Credit Union National Association, Rayovac Corporation and P.H. Glatfelter Paper.